Praise for

The Karma Queens' Guide to Relationships

"*The Karma Queens' Guide to Relationships* is an essential compass and guide to attract and navigate authentic, passionate, and loving relationships. Carmen Harra has masterfully and compassionately revealed the source of a fulfilled and meaningful life . . . the ability to consciously love and be loved. I highly recommend this book!"

> —**Dr. Darren R. Weissman,** author of *The Heart of the Matter*
> and *Awakening the Secret Code of Your Mind*

"Carmen Harra has done it again! *The Karma Queens' Guide to Relationships* not only reveals the influence our past lives have on our present relationships, it also shows us what to do to reverse our negative patterns and awaken to unlimited love and joy."

> —**Sandra Anne Taylor,** *New York Times*–bestselling
> author of *Quantum Success*

"*The Karma Queens' Guide to Relationships* offers a brand-new perspective on relationships, proving that karma is the number-one driving force behind the human dynamic."

> —**Colette Baron Reid,** author of *Weight Loss for People*
> *Who Feel Too Much* and *The Map: Finding the Magic*
> *and Meaning in the Story of Your Life*

The

KARMA QUEENS'

Guide to

Relationships

JEREMY P. TARCHER/PENGUIN
a member of Penguin Group (USA)
New York

The

KARMA QUEENS'

Guide to

Relationships

*The Truth about Karma
and Relationships*

CARMEN HARRA, PhD,
and ALEXANDRA HARRA

JEREMY P. TARCHER/PENGUIN
Published by the Penguin Group
Penguin Group (USA) LLC
375 Hudson Street
New York, New York 10014

USA • Canada • UK • Ireland • Australia
New Zealand • India • South Africa • China

penguin.com
A Penguin Random House Company

Most Tarcher/Penguin books are available at special quantity discounts for
bulk purchase for sales promotions, premiums, fund-raising, and educational
needs. Special books or book excerpts also can be created to fit specific
needs. For details, write: Special.Markets@us.penguingroup.com.

Library of Congress Cataloging-in-Publication Data

Harra, Carmen.
The karma queens' guide to relationships : the truth about karma and
relationships / Carmen Harra, PhD, and Alexandra Harra.
p.   cm.
ISBN 978-0-399-17390-5
1. Interpersonal relations.   2. Friendship.   3. Karma.
I. Harra, Alexandra.   II. Title
HM1106.H369   2015   2015002868
302—dc23

Printed in the United States of America
1   3   5   7   9   10   8   6   4   2

BOOK DESIGN BY AMANDA DEWEY

I dedicate this book to my friends, family members, and clients, whose unique stories added to my understanding of the divine nature of relationships.

CONTENTS

INTRODUCTION

*On every path of life there can be found
traces of karmic footprints.*

—DR. CARMEN HARRA AND
ALEXANDRA HARRA

CARMEN HARRA, PhD

Virgil

On the day of my father's funeral, through my tears and broken spirit, I received a message that would forever change my life. I suddenly saw the spirit of my father standing beside his own grave. "Look at the headstone behind mine," he told me. "On it is the name of your future husband."

I was single at the time, a celebrated singer in Romania, and utterly devastated by the recent loss of my beloved father, Victor. He had always been kind, loving, and supportive, even when I insisted that I wanted to be a professional singer in the midst of the communist regime (and he was wise enough to give me his blessings on the condition that I get a college degree as a backup).

When I saw the name *Virgil* imprinted into the gravestone behind his, I committed it to memory. I knew I could trust my father's guidance and the otherworldly advice that came from loved ones who had crossed over and given me signs and insights about my future. I had been told that someday I—a girl who had spent her early childhood in a one-room house without running water, and grown to adulthood in an Eastern Bloc country where freedom was a tantalizing dream—would go to America and be on television. It was crazy to think this could happen—people said that often enough! But I held on to this beautiful dream with fervent tenacity.

Exactly seven days after my father died and three days after I received the message at his gravesite, I was in America with a touring company of performers. It was a trip I had been looking forward to for many months and an utterly bittersweet moment. I was excited to achieve my dream at last, but deeply saddened about having just lost a parent. How I would have loved to share with my father the story of my adventure in New York City, singing at last in front of an American audience! But my father's presence, it turns out, was far from gone. He was working in mysterious ways from the other side to forever solidify my fate.

After my performance, an extremely handsome man walked up to me and introduced himself as Virgil, the event coordinator. My jaw dropped as he started to talk about his restaurant and wanting to book me to sing there. I had to sit down, afraid that I would keel over. I knew without a doubt that this was the Virgil my father had prophesied. My mind was suddenly flooded with flashbacks: visions of the lives we had spent together in other times and other lands. I saw it all so clearly. Virgil had died in my arms in Israel, hundreds of years ago, in the midst of a civil uprising. Just as in that lifetime, he was destined to die prematurely once more. I knew it from the moment I saw him. It wasn't pleasant, but it was our karma. And Virgil was my soul mate.

A few days later, Virgil proposed and three weeks later, we were married. How crazy is that? But he and I shared the most loving, enriching relationship for twenty-seven years. Perhaps it never would have happened if it hadn't been for my father and his timely guidance from the world beyond our own.

Our meeting was karmic, no doubt. We were meant to spend our lives together, and my father on the other side had known this. I felt it when I met Virgil, and he felt it with me. When two people are meant to be together, that sense of instant connection can be incredibly powerful. It's almost inexplicable. And our destiny codes—determined by numerology—validated what Virgil and I felt with each other.

Over the years, my husband and I met brutal challenges in our relationship, as all couples do. I married a man with two young daughters who almost overnight had to adjust to having a stepmother. Virgil and I went into business together running another restaurant, and anyone who has mixed business and family knows the problems it can cause! But fortunately, our conflicts weren't serious enough to threaten the relationship, and we worked through them with mutual effort. The two of us were determined to make our marriage happy and create positive karma together. On the day of his death, Virgil's last words to me were that he would "see me soon." I can only hope that in my next life on earth, Virgil and I find each other again as twin souls who search for their missing half.

We knew, as too many don't, that being honest about our failings and balancing our personal needs with the needs of the other was crucial to our success as a couple. We had excellent role models in our families—again, an advantage many aren't fortunate enough to have. We kept guard against creating bad karma—saying or doing things to each other we would later regret, for instance. We were also careful not to let other people's karma influence our relationship. Our families were incredibly important to each of us, but their interference was walled off from our private relationship.

Virgil encouraged me to become a counselor, and for many years I have helped people both in my role as a licensed clinical psychologist and as an intuitive counselor. Because of my own experiences and beliefs, I teach my clients not to end difficult relationships or cut off relatives whose behavior irritates or angers them, except as a last resort. I know that karma will compel them to enter new relationships that will display the same problems that were present in the old relationships. Those with whom we create a rift are likely to show up again in this life or the next, or the next, until our shared karma is resolved (and yes, we share karma with others, as you'll learn). We may escape this life and its circumstances, even shed our bodies as our souls move from life to life, but there is no escaping our karma.

The single greatest positive step you can take toward personal progress is to stop ignoring your karma and start mastering it. Then you can become a karma queen (or king) who no longer lives according to the dictates of karma created long ago.

ALEXANDRA HARRA

....

My Mother, Queen of What?

Growing up, we all have a little bit of trouble understanding our parents: the weird things they do, like file taxes and argue over the phone about their credit card interest rate. But I had particular trouble understanding what exactly my mother did for a living. All I knew was that she saw clients in her office and they always cried because they suddenly understood the meaning of life or their deceased aunt came through via my mom's mediumship abilities. I was confused, at best. My friends at school would brag about their parents' jobs (cops and lawyers and presidents of companies) and I would just shrug and say, "Well, my mom's The Karma Queen."

"What's that?" they'd ask.

"I'm still trying to figure it out," I would respond.

The *New York Post* bestowed her with the title in 2003. Sixteen at the time and brimming with youthful ignorance, I didn't yet understand the fact that karma accounted for my attraction to all the bad boys at school, my phobia of big ships, and my lack of self-esteem as a child. Only as the years passed did I inherit the wisdom of The Karma Queen, drop by drop, day by day, until the pieces of the puzzle fell into place with resounding self-awareness. I was finally in possession of my true self, understanding my faults, weaknesses, and tendencies as well as their karmic origins.

I learned what my mom's unique job title meant through time

and daily exposure to the karma of others. I not only learned about her work, I came to revere it. Beginning in my early teenage years, I visited many of my mom's clients with her and became familiar with their stories. I started to have a strong empathy for people, becoming sensitive to their needs and wants without even realizing it. I would listen, and their words would affect me as if their history were my own. I peered into their lives as a stranger who was filled with curiosity, and often recognized truths they were blind to because of their overwhelming emotion and strong will. It got to the point that when my mom would speak to her clients, I would innocently chime in with my own, somewhat intuitive advice. I may have had chutzpah stepping in that way, but my mother and her clients saw the validity of what I was saying.

So how could all that wisdom come from someone who simultaneously battled her own demons? Well, for one thing, it came from watching my mom work, but my degree in classics also helped—all things repeat in time, so what has happened before is bound to happen again. When you understand this, you can anticipate the outcome to most events. Most important, I recognized that I was an old soul with karma from previous lifetimes and a talent for understanding people. As the saying goes, "It is both a blessing and a curse to feel everything so deeply." I'm grateful to be able to feel what others feel—their tumultuous and sometimes terrible thoughts. I'm grateful because I can feel their karma.

By listening to thousands of different cases, I learned that we all walk down the same roads, only we travel at our own pace and leave different footprints behind. The stories of our lives share undeniable similarities, but what makes your life experiences unique to you is your individual karma, the record of your soul's deeds and debts to the universe. And if you shed your fears and probe into your karmic record, you can find out the reason behind many of your circumstances. As Virgil the Roman poet said, "Happy is he who has been able to learn the causes of things." What's more, if you are willing not only to acknowledge your karma but take the extra step and act to resolve it, you can make true progress in every relationship and aspect of life. A karmic cleanse of all those karmic toxins you've accumulated will help you move forward.

Having experienced my own glorious karmic coming-of-age, I am ready to take the spiritual baton from my mother and become the next Karma Queen.

CARMEN

What's in Your Suitcase?

Karma is like a suitcase you carry with you everywhere—only, unlike suitcases you bring to the airport, it never gets lost! That's not always such a good thing. . . . If you want to lighten your load and experience greater joy, you have to be curious and courageous enough to open that suitcase (painful as that may be), sort through its contents, and get rid of what you don't need—particularly patterns that will poison your relationships. When you have unresolved karma, you think you've left behind your demanding mother, but you marry a demanding man, or find yourself working for a demanding boss. Or one day you are telling your teenager what to do and she shouts, "Mom, you are so demanding!" and you wonder, "What happened to me? I've turned into my mother and I always swore I wouldn't!" What happened is that you thought there was a simple solution to the discomfort of the conflict between you and your mother: avoid her and repress your irritation. Instead, you inadvertently set up complications in future relationships, because they would be affected by past karma that you failed to resolve.

And you aren't the only one who brings a suitcase of karma into any particular relationship. It was no accident that you were attracted to a spouse who asks for too much, or the job with the demanding boss. They, too, had karma that attracted them to you so that you and they could cooperate and work to resolve the outstanding karma and generate new, more positive karma. And your child or children were born to you knowing your karma before they ever entered into this world, and wanting to resolve karma of their own carried over from a past life. It's all outlined in our karmic contract, which we sign as souls on the other side before reentering the physical world. We forget this contract once our soul enters a body and must rediscover its contents the harder way, through experience.

Unlike breaking a contract with a dealership or mortgage company, breaking a karmic contract has greater repercussions than just monetary penalties. Failing to resolve your unique karma as stated in your soul contract means not learning the lessons you were put on earth to learn. And that means you don't become fulfilled, your life stagnates, and you have to come back to this physical life over and over until you finally finish what you came to do. To triumph over your karma is a challenge, yes, but then again, what is more rewarding than conquering a personal challenge?

My daughter Alexandra had a karmic relationship with her ex-boyfriend (she's rolling her eyes right now). They were together for five painstaking years (painstaking for her, joyful for him). Because their relationship was karmic (you'll learn more about that type of relationship later), it was intense. Alexandra shifted between being protective of her boyfriend and being demanding of him, and would explain to me, "Mom, he and I have a karmic connection. In a past life, he was my servant, I was wealthy, and I was very cruel to him. Now I feel like I owe him." She was trying to work with him through that karmic dynamic in this life, and I'm glad she was committed to doing that.

I am not glad, however, to remember the amount of money it cost us.

Yes, I know that what I'm describing is not your typical mother-daughter conversation about boyfriends, but that's the way Alexandra and I talk to each other. We're kindred spirits as much as mother and daughter. She has learned a lot from me. Ever since she was a little girl, she has been very observant of people. But she also has a gift for insight that is karmic.

Alexandra knew that her relationship was a karmic one and that she had to be mindful of her behavior patterns and dedicated to changing them. It also meant I had to deal with her and her ex-boyfriend's dramas playing out in front of me in our home, and hold back from giving her—and him—advice. This was especially difficult considering that as a licensed clinical psychologist, I could easily see the mistakes they were making—and as a meta-physical intuitive, I knew the relationship wasn't going to last. Yet I had to respect their choice to be in the relationship, working to detangle their karma.

Working through karma can be very onerous. Clearing old karma can take a long time. Think about clearing the contents of a very old house in which you've lived your entire life—there will be ancient stashes of stuff you long forgot you even had. But coming across old photographs and clothes and trinkets will bring back submerged memories and an understanding of how far you've come since then. That's what digging through your karmic suitcase does: it makes you aware of what you've worked on and what still requires work. Patience with the process is essential. If you give up quickly out of frustration, you're just going to end up dealing with the same issues, only in a different relationship. But when you push through and make progress, ah! Then you feel yourself being liberated. You feel yourself mastering your karma, and there is no more powerful feeling than knowing you are in control.

By resolving your karma, by bringing love and patience into the situation and acting from your highest, most evolved and spiritual self, you end the cycle of going from one similar relationship to another and repeating the old patterns that bring you and others pain. You open yourself up to attract new people into your life—a romantic partner, a new group of friends, a business or creative partner who complements you perfectly, or a neighbor who makes life much more pleasant. Resolving your karma and becoming a master over it involves some discomfort. You're going to have to look at yourself honestly with all your flaws, and address your behaviors and your hidden thoughts that drive them. The payoff is that you will become much happier and more at peace with yourself and your relationships.

Relationships are the ground on which we resolve our old karma, because they are the way through which karma manifests itself. They make us into karma queens if we don't run from the work that relationships require. Whether they are with someone we love or someone we can't stand but can't avoid, relationships cause us simultaneous pain and joy. Our patterns depend on what is in our karmic luggage.

If you want to stop suffering and heal your relationships so that they are supportive, loving, and nurturing, you must stop focusing on the problems other people cause you and start looking at yourself. What is the only common element in every relationship you have? You! You're in every relationship, and you bring to it a suitcase full of karma that you, and only you, can sort through. If you do so, your relationships will be less complicated and much more rewarding.

The lesson is that you must stop trying to change others' karma. Change your own instead!

And once you find the courage to look at your role in all your relationships, and you see what you need to change, you have to follow through on working on your karma at every opportunity. You must remain honest with yourself and take time to reflect. Throughout this book, you'll find exercises and activities that can help you with this process.

The Karmic Cure

In addition to the mental, emotional, and practical work you need to do within your relationships to resolve karma, you must do energy work. You must use the energy of love—the karmic cure for your relationships.

Love is the most powerful force in the universe. You must love others, of course, but never forget that you must love yourself also. Otherwise, you won't find the courage to keep working on your issues. As Jesus said, "Love your neighbor as you love yourself." However, this won't work unless you love yourself first. As the Bible also says, "Remove the plank in your own eye before trying to remove the speck in your neighbor's." Resolve your own karma and you will much more easily affect other people's behavior. You can't force others to change, but by changing yourself, you transform your relationship dynamics. That's the beginning of becoming a karma queen who reigns over her karma.

To master your karma, you have to start with yourself and your issues—and even if your main concern is your romantic relationship, you have to look at the full spectrum of your relationships and your part in them. You also have to consider the karmic and energetic influences on your relationships—all of which you will learn about in these chapters. You will hear from both me and Alexandra in our own words and in our combined voice at times. We really do finish each other's sentences, and we're very much in agreement on most everything (just not men, spending habits, or hair color). So the advice here comes from two souls profoundly in sync who want to offer you the greatest range of guidance.

As the stars of our own reality television series appropriately titled *Karma Queens*, we found this to be the perfect time to share our combined knowledge of karma and relationships. We want to help you understand your bonds from a completely new perspective—a karmic one. Through our separate voices, bridging the generation gap, and accepting and integrating each other's different ideas, we feel we can advise you on how to cultivate relationships that fill your spirit with joy, just as they were meant to.

Every relationship in your life will present dilemmas and conflicts. You can deny the problems, or get into arguments or battles with others and try to dominate or conquer them, or you can apply the karmic cure of love and modify your thoughts and actions. If you choose the karmic cure, your relationships will enhance your life. Studies show that a strong social circle leads to better health and greater longevity. As a child of God, you deserve to be loved, cherished, and cared for by others just as you are loved, cherished, and cared for by God. We were meant to extend the infinite love we receive from the Divine to each other.

We hope this book, written from our hearts, helps you to master your karma—to become queens (or kings) of your karma—and to receive the unconditional love that is your unwavering birthright.

BECOMING A "KARMA QUEEN"

(Mastering Your Karma So Your Relationships Don't Drive You Crazy)

Mastering your karma is mastering your life.

—DR. CARMEN HARRA

CARMEN

The Origin of the Karma Queens

My grandmother passed while giving birth to my mother, Alexandrina (after whom Alexandra is named). Sanda, as we called her for short, was then raised by her father, sisters, and brothers, and never felt that one-of-a-kind love from a mother. In turn, when she had my younger sister and me, Sanda wasn't sure how to balance being too protective with being too permissive. The karma she experienced by never having a mother figure led her to develop a strong fear of losing us. She acted on this fear by being extremely protective and possessive. No matter what friends or, later, boyfriends we brought home, Sanda disliked them all. My mom had to accompany us everywhere, far beyond our teenage years.

I remember being twenty-four years old, a famous singer in Romania on tour with my band . . . and also my mother, who had to come along to make sure no one harmed me in any way (she would give all men my age the old evil eye so that no one dared approach me). As I was a normal young woman with a desire for a relationship, this made me miserable. But I don't fault her for her behavior—it was all Sanda knew. My mother never addressed the karmic issues created by not having had a motherly role model to learn from. This is what happens when we don't take an honest look at our karma and act to resolve it—we repeat it, and not just in our own lives. We transfer it to others, affecting their lives, too.

I admit that even I acted on the karma between my mother and me in my treatment of my youngest daughter, Alexandra, except I verged on the other extreme. I was afraid that Alexandra would grow to resent me if I was too controlling of her as my mother had been of me. So I became a lenient parent . . . so lenient that I took Alexandra to get her first tattoo at age fourteen. Yes, I know, how could I have done that? I didn't recognize my karma in time! If I had, I probably would have made a different decision and changed the pattern of letting my daughter have too much freedom at such a young age. I had learned much about karma and karmic relationships, but I still had to overcome the karma I had inherited from my own mother.

Luckily for Alexandra and me, we realized that we are different people and that there's no need to play on each other's weaknesses or act out our personal insecurities. On the contrary, we work best as a team, so together, we're working to master the hefty mother-daughter karma in our family line (we've been working on this for quite a while now, so Alexandra stopped getting tattoos and I stopped letting her). I've learned to be tougher on her and she's learned to be less of a rebel. There's no need to let the old karma of my mother, or her mother before her, or my former mistakes as a mother, get between Alexandra and me. We are committed to cooperating with each other and lifting each other up. In this way, we heal and resolve the old karma, mastering its lessons instead of letting its lessons master us.

I have been dubbed The Karma Queen because this concept of karma is central to my work as a licensed clinical psychologist and intuitive advisor and coach. It is also central to my books, and even to the jewelry I design. It was karma that led me to become a singer, which turned out to be my ticket to freedom from the communist regime I lived under in my younger years. And now my daughter, Alexandra, is becoming a karma queen. She has learned that if you don't preside over your karma, it will dominate most aspects of your life.

As I said, my own mother was very possessive of my sister, Mona, and me. Mona is a lesbian (sexuality has karmic roots, too!), but our mother's behavior toward us is key to why Mona decided not to have children or adopt: she held resentment against her mother for her choice of parenting and this discouraged her from wanting to become a parent herself. I was affected in the way that I verged on the opposite extreme and let my daughter,

Alexandra, get away with most anything. Now, Alexandra and I have worked out our karma very well, though she doesn't have children yet, so I can't say what her mothering approach will be!

The much-needed balance in parent-child dynamics came into our family through my two stepdaughters, Carmen and Florina. Each has two children, a total of two boys and two girls, and in studying their treatment of their children, I can say I've seen truly balanced mothering in action—they are neither too strict nor too lenient. This is what I dream of for Alexandra and her children, if and when she becomes a mother. Though they are much younger than me, Carmen and Florina taught me a lesson I couldn't have learned elsewhere—the lesson of how to discipline your children and protect them without going overboard and becoming domineering. You see, it is one thing to learn discipline in books and coursework as a therapist. It is another thing to experience the idea of balanced discipline by observing it expressed again and again. I now have internalized a more balanced approach to interacting with my own daughter. When I look at my stepdaughters with their children, I see their sons and daughters clinging to them and relying on them, and at the same time showing respect and not rebelling against them for no reason but ego and will.

Such balance was something I had to work hard through many years to achieve with Alexandra because I had no example of it, only an idea of balance as something for which to strive. Our family's story of mothers and daughters shows that the effects of shared karma are both real and profound.

If you're not aware of your karma and how it affects all the relationships in your life . . . well, let me explain how it all works.

The True Nature of Karma

Long before we are born, we begin to create relationships and, consequently, karmic ties. You are karmically linked to your mother, of course, who gave birth to you, and to your father because you are his product. To a lesser degree, you are karmically linked to the doctor who delivered you, the kindergarten teacher who scolded you, your first boyfriend or girlfriend who broke your heart (or whose heart you broke), and so on. You go through life creating karma, resolving it, creating it, resolving it, until your body is ready to expire and your soul ascends to the higher realm. The hope is that by then, all of your karma will have been healed and rectified. But because we are not aware of our true karmic nature, this is rarely the case. And so our soul returns in the flesh once more in its next life on earth. And what has remained unchecked on the karmic to-do list is picked up again. This brings you to here and now. Do you know what's on your soul's to-do list?

Karma is a much-misunderstood concept. It's not quite as simple as "what goes around comes around" or "how you treat others is how they will treat you." The Sanskrit word *karma* means the force of thoughts and deeds. This energy manifests as beliefs, emotions, and actions. The energy of karma becomes woven into your personal energy field, or consciousness. It gets attached to the soul and remains there lifetime after lifetime until it is resolved. In a way, it's like a tattoo that can't be removed without a lot of work (something Alexandra has come to appreciate and abhor . . .). Action creates memory, and karma is the memory of the soul.

The doors of infinite possibilities open when you acknowledge your karma and heal or resolve it. You must accept three truths about karma: that it is the accumulation of every thought, intention, and action from this and prior lifetimes, that it can always be healed, and that healing requires action.

The First Truth about Karma: Karma Is the Accumulation of Every Thought, Intention, and Action from This and Prior Lifetimes

Whatever actions you take have lasting effects because everything in the universe is energy, and everything is connected in the field of energy. It's like what happens when you drop a stone into a pool of still water: ripples emanate. You can watch them move outward, rocking a small stick on the water's surface and changing the reflection of the sky on the water. All of your actions send waves of energy outward, affecting others in ways greater than you can imagine. Some actions create bad karma because you are hurting others, whether you know it or not. But if your actions are loving and kind—and make others feel happy, at peace, loved, and valued—then you are generating excellent karma. Having a clean karmic record frees your spirit.

You can't always see the far-reaching, long-lasting effects of the karma you've generated, but the memory becomes part of the consciousness of the individuals involved as well as part of the collective consciousness of the universe that our individual minds are connected to. The parent who couldn't express unconditional love to you when you were a baby created bad karma, which was stored in you as a memory that may have been forgotten by your conscious mind but was held in your unconscious mind and your body's energy field, and even etched into your brain. This subconscious memory can resurface at any given moment if the right situation presents itself.

You see, each time you experience a thought or emotion, neurons in your brain fire off electrical impulses that create or reinforce dendrites, or arms, that reach from one neuron to another. You reuse this neural network or path because it's easier than creating a new one. But if the old path is the path of jealousy, vindictiveness, distrust, or anxiety, you'll habitually experience those feelings—and thoughts that support them—unless you forge a new path. Bridges must be burned to erect new ones.

Sometimes when you are driving, you can find you're headed home when you meant to go to the store. When you get distracted, your mind can go on autopilot. It will efficiently send you onto the road to your home without your realizing it because you're not paying attention. The same thing happens in your relationships: you stumble down the same road. You find yourself not speaking up when you're feeling disrespected, or you start arguments about something inconsequential to avoid talking about what's really bothering you. The karma you create by not being honest with yourself and your partner, and by not working through the real problems, accumulates. Again and again, you find yourself being uncomfortable and challenged to resolve your karma. And if you continue to operate on "autopilot" in these uncomfortable situations, you will continue to meet the same uncomfortable results.

The Second Truth about Karma:
Karma Can Always Be Healed

Changing your karma is far easier and more sensible than trying to change other people. Transforming karma is difficult and requires much time and effort. First, however, you have to become aware of it. That means allowing yourself to feel embarrassed or even ashamed and defensive. Your ego will try to keep you from admitting that you play a role in all your problems. It's easier to blame your spouse, your daughter, your parent, or your coworker. Deep down, perhaps you will feel a twinge of guilt when you vent about someone who upset you. Pay attention to that feeling and listen to that voice inside that says, "Yes, but what about what you did?" It is impossible to control what others do, but if you master your karma, you can control how you feel, act, and think. This, in turn, will affect how others behave toward you.

And second, you have to *remain* aware of your karma, or you will find yourself on the wrong road, thinking, "How did I get here? I meant to go somewhere else!" You must develop the habit of being both mindful and reflective. If you are constantly thinking about tomorrow or last week, or what happened ten years ago, or what might happen "if only that person would change," you're not being mindful of how you are perpetuating your karma.

Third, you have to understand your karma's nature and origins. In this way, you can appreciate why it's so powerful and become more accepting of yourself and others. It is not easy to change karma, so don't harshly judge yourself or the people you care about. As you'll learn, your karma may have been created in a previous lifetime and carried over to this one—it may even be so strong that you've held on to it for several lifetimes with little or no awareness.

You can become aware of your karma and commit yourself to creating new, good karma that heals old, bad karma—but you have to do more than *intend* to change your habits. You actually have to change your habits. You have to act and resolve your karma. Then the people around you will act differently in response. True, they may drift away or end the relationship with you because they still have karma of their own to resolve and they aren't ready to change. Or the way in which you've changed—becoming stronger, more aware, and more enlightened—may frustrate them and cause them to end their relationship with you. Most people don't like it when you no longer conform to them. If so, rest assured that you'll find new people who will come into your life—people who may be much more supportive of the new you who stands up for yourself and is honest about your own failings. The Law of Attraction, one of the eleven divine laws that I, Carmen, wrote about in my book *The Eleven Eternal Principles*, states that like attracts like—so when *you* transform, your *relationships* transform. This is just one of the positive results of change.

The Third Truth about Karma: Healing Karma Requires Action

"I'm stuck" is a phrase heard every day in our office as clients come to find solutions for their problems. We sympathize with their challenges and relate to their suffering. It's hard to watch when they repeat the same mistakes over and over. They admit that what they most often struggle with is falling victim to unwanted repetitions of old patterns.

Time is fluid, but while it can't stand still, we can and sometimes do enter periods of stagnancy. This is normal, and these times provide opportunities for reflecting on what we've learned and planning what we want to do next, but they can be very frustrating. We want our lives to be happy all the time, but that's not possible. Sometimes we have to experience pain to learn our life lessons. The pain inspires us to take appropriate action. The actions we must take all depend on what we must do to simplify and lighten our karmic load.

Most of us don't act in the right time. We cause ourselves more suffering by acting in the wrong time. We don't understand the concept of divine timing and force things to happen when they're not meant to. We break things off and experience immense anguish, or we push ourselves toward the wrong move, all because we're desperate to act. We wrongly think, "If it doesn't happen now, it'll never happen." Instead, we should wait for the karmic wheel to come around in our favor. When the Divine gives you every indication that timing is in your favor—act! For the love of God, act! But until then, be silent and faithful.

It's easy to become trapped in recurring cycles—for instance, attracting the same type of people into your life—if you haven't yet addressed your karma with action. It may be one demanding boss after another, a series of abusive partners, or a slew of unfaithful friends, but we all have that one type of person who just keeps popping up in our lives. If your partner betrays you, you swear never to date a cheater again. Yet somehow you draw in a lover who manifests the same behaviors as your ex-partner—and you don't take action by breaking it off. Or you may feel surrounded by emotionally exhausting people and just don't know how to escape their energetic trap, so you maintain the relationships and do nothing to make them better. When you realize this is happening, it's time to clean out the old karmic suitcase you're dragging around.

It's painful to cut off patterns of relationships, especially if you've become attached to someone. But remember that it only hurts once and never has to hurt again, as you are ready to bring in new types of people with whom you can foster healthier relationships. You have to be good to yourself even as you're being honest with yourself about your weaknesses, and then you have to create good karma in your relationships. You have to balance the karmic books, so to speak.

You see, just as you don't want to have outstanding monetary debt, you also don't want to have outstanding karmic debt. Karmic debt complicates your life and keeps you in patterns of behavior for so long you might even forget how they got started. You "overspend" by taking from other people and treating them badly because you're distracted or insecure, or minimizing how much you hurt them with your words, and then you end up overdrawn at the karmic bank. The bad karma you've accumulated becomes greater than the favorable karma you've generated. Constricted by karmic debt, you cannot measure the full breadth of life.

You've seen this in relationships, haven't you? A friend stuns another by abruptly ending their long friendship, or a spouse walks out of a marriage saying, "I've been unhappy for a long time and you haven't been listening," sending the other spouse into shock. When the balance between two people is lost and one's karmic debt to the other is too great, the relationship often breaks under the strain. Then the karmic debt is brought over into the next relationship—and this is true for both partners. Even if you were the one who was wronged (from your perspective), your unwillingness to stand up for yourself created bad karma that hurt you. The bad karma will carry over into your next relationship if you don't begin to master your karma.

Relationships: It's Complicated!

When a relationship is confusing and dramatic, marked by extreme ups and downs, we sigh and say, "It's complicated." But we're the ones who complicate our relationships by not resolving our karma. And the way to uncomplicate relationships and smooth out the bumps is to employ a karmic cure: love.

Love is universal. Love is your birthright. And love is what makes you be good to yourself and others no matter how complicated a relationship seems at any time. Choose love and you begin to heal the bad karma you have created with others. Your relationships will become less complex and return to the simple joys that are meant to mark the human bond.

You may be focused only on the relationship that's giving you grief right now, and thinking, "If I can just fix this relationship, everything will be okay." However, if you step back from the situation and reflect, becoming painfully honest with yourself, it's not just this relationship that's a problem. All your relationships are intertwined, and the karma you create in them carries over to your other bonds.

Love extends far beyond romantic relationships. There's familial love, parent/child love, the love you share with close friends, love you share with people around you who live nearby or work with you, and love you have for strangers simply because, like you, they're just people trying to live happily. And of course, there's love for our animal companions. This abundance of love has the potential to inspire us to create wonderful karma. But because our egos cause us to be scared of losing love, or not being loved, or not being lovable, we react on our fears and create bad karma—even when we're with those we love most.

Love is the foundation of all relationships, and relationships exist so that we can learn to choose love over fear, anger, and insecurity. The more love you have in your relationships, the more you will thrive—and the more others will survive. In a perfect world, everyone would get along all the time. Unfortunately, we easily fall prey to suspicion, jealousy, and fear. Our relationships become turbulent and complex. We find ourselves enmeshed with someone we don't even like, and can't figure out why it's so hard to break off the connection. Or we love someone so much we can't imagine living without them, but we cause that person pain. Families can be torn apart by conflict as sister is pitted against sister, and the mother is torn apart by her loyalties to all her children. Resolving the karma of all relationships means starting from the beginning and tracing your karmic line back to the relationship you experienced with your parents, in particular your mother.

Many mothers have trouble fostering a healthy relationship with their daughters. Women often define themselves by their relationships, so the primary female relationship, the mother-daughter bond, is the most intense relationship that exists. And it can be very turbulent! That's because within that intensity it's difficult to maintain your own identity.

It's common for a daughter to want to avoid "becoming" her mother, yet she knows she would not be here if it were not for her mother—and her mother's influence is powerful even if they are not close. And with daughters, there's always a hint of subconscious competition with Mom. Often, a daughter who has a rough relationship with her mother will have problems with the man in her life. Or the cycle will repeat and she'll unknowingly behave with her daughter as her own mother behaved with her, causing the same kinds of issues. Sometimes she repeats the behavior her mother exhibited, and sometimes she reverts to the behavior she exhibited when she clashed with her own mother.

As a mother and daughter, Alexandra and I see our relationship as a prime garden for healing our karma. We try to remember that fact, even when we're so mad at each other we could scream! The reality is that the more strongly connected you are to someone emotionally, the more you are challenged by the discomfort of conflict. As you know, relationships offer the opportunity to become master of one's karma. To reduce drama in your life, you must give up being a drama queen and become a karma queen—and yes, we are all drama queens at times (some of us more than others, admittedly).

When most people hear the word *relationship*, they think of romantic relationships, which can be very intense. In fact, the self-help shelf is full of books on these sorts of relationships. Rare is the book that covers relationships other than the romantic kind. This is understandable, for if you are deeply in love with someone, it's incredibly painful if you're in conflict with that person. You want help! However—and this is extremely important!—it's very distorted to focus on the primary relationship of a marriage or long-term committed partnership and forget all the others. A dysfunctional relationship with a close friend, a parent, or an adult child can put so much pressure on a marriage that it leads to divorce. A troubled relationship with a business or creative partner can cause severe stress in your personal life as well.

That said, if you choose to resolve karma within those relationships, it will only improve your marriage and all your other relationships. All relationships are sewn together in our human experience, and to untangle only one and think you're free from the karmic net simply won't work. The Law of Unity, one of the eleven eternal principles, states that we are all interconnected. The bad karma in a dynamic between you and one other person isn't contained. It spills out and affects your other relationships. That's why we have deliberately chosen to make this book about being more self-aware in—and resolving karma in—*all* of your relationships. That may sound radical, but it really is the core of healing karma and the road to a happier life.

Shared Karma

Each of us has unresolved karma that we share with a group of people, such as with a family or community. A family can share a karmic issue of abandonment that carries over from lifetime to lifetime and generation to generation. The United States has bad karma generated back when Americans enslaved African Americans, murdered and exploited Native Americans, and stripped Japanese Americans of their property and imprisoned them in camps during World War II. Romania, where I, Carmen, was born and raised, has bad karma from killing so many of its leaders over the years and persecuting minorities. Families have karma that follow them from lifetime to lifetime. Fortunately, in each new lifetime, every individual and every group is given opportunity after opportunity to resolve the old, bad karma; draw upon the karmic experiences of the past; and generate new, good karma through the force of love. The law of karma is fair. Karma really isn't a you-know-what, after all.

Are you personally responsible for what your ancestors did? Are you responsible for what your fellow citizens did in the distant past, when your own family immigrated to the United States a few years ago? Not necessarily, but it may be that in a past life, you were involved in the mistreatment of others and you have karma to work through. Remember that our souls have taken on many forms before, and we carry over unresolved karma from previous lives.

While it can be helpful to use hypnotism to learn about past lives and karma you generated long ago, keep in mind that if you create positive karma now and in the future, you can erase bad karma. You don't have to know its origins in past lives, but it is helpful to know where the issues first arose in this life. Often, the work of resolving karma begins with identifying your own psychological issues (or, as they're called in cognitive therapy, *core schemas*) and observing how they play out. After that, it takes vigilance to remain observant and make new decisions each time a situation comes up and an opportunity for changing habits presents itself. It's especially difficult with the old issues that go back several lifetimes. Mastering karma is not easy, but it can absolutely be done.

Karmic issues can manifest in different types of relationships and in different forms. If you were abandoned by your father, you may end up abandoning your wife instead of your child. You may not see it this way—you might think, "I'm nothing like my father! He was terrible!" Yet part of you knows you have repeated his behavior in a slightly different way. Vowing not to be like the one who harmed you is not enough. You must resolve the old, bad karma that you carry with you or you will manifest it in your life.

All karmic issues will play out in your life in some way. And they may have effects that last for many incarnations of your own life or your group's, and many generations of your descendants. The karma that we refuse to address, unfortunately, the next in line may have to resolve.

Karma, Carried Over

To better understand karma and how it clings to us, you must understand that although each of us has a mind, a set of memories, a personality or temperament, and a body, our true nature is energetic. We are souls, or energy beings, that have consciousness. Consciousness can be transformed, but, like all forms of energy, it can never be destroyed. Our individual consciousness is connected to all the consciousness in the universe—the consciousness of people who lived long ago, the consciousness of souls yet to be born, and the consciousness of God or Spirit. It is the soul that bears the imprint of karma. The soul transmigrates, moving from body, to separation from form after we die, to a new body as we reincarnate, to the spirit world—the cycle repeats again and again until all karma has been resolved. In several past lives, I, Carmen, and Virgil were romantic partners, and in previous lives, Alexandra and I were sisters. (I, Alexandra, am convinced I was also my mom's mom in a previous life, but she has trouble admitting this, because it means I got to tell her what to do.)

When we are in the form of souls existing in the realm of Spirit, unattached from bodies, we choose to take human form to experience life on this planet. We do this in order to resolve our karma and learn our lessons. Our consciousness directs the formation of the baby in the womb, including its DNA and its brain, and we infuse it with our consciousness when the baby's body is ready to receive it. All our memories of past lives become buried in the subconscious mind—packed away in the suitcase, so to speak. The conscious mind develops and learns as a result of our adventures on earth, but it doesn't easily access the information in the subconscious mind. It is unaware of its connection, through the portal of the subconscious mind, with all consciousness.

As we mature into adulthood, we might become consciously aware of our karma, or it might remain hidden in our subconscious for our entire lives. Either way, it affects us. When we die, the division between our conscious and unconscious disappears and we reclaim all our memories of the past, including our past lives. We do a life review. All our karma remains as a memory and an energetic imprint on the soul.

However, unlike when we are on earth, we don't feel any negative emotions when we examine our karma on the other side. Fear, anger, resentment, sadness, and jealousy have a low vibration, and once we have shed our bodies and returned to the spiritual realm, our vibration is too high for us to experience these feelings. We are able to look at the past and our karma without shame, fear, or embarrassment, and we decide what we want to experience in the next life in order to resolve it.

In mediumship sessions, spirits on the other side who come through no longer feel anger, resentment, or insecurity. They're always remorseful for the mistakes they made. They ask the living for forgiveness.

Is it hard to imagine that on the other side, you will look back at the cruelest thing you ever did to another, or the most painful loss you suffered in this lifetime, and feel no shame, sadness, or regret? Karma is emotional baggage or luggage that lasts through several lifetimes. On the other side, you can unpack your karmic suitcase, survey what you have, and plan how you will resolve your karma when you return to earth. However, you won't feel any heavy, earthly emotions like shame, fear, or anger as you examine your karma. Only on earth will you experience the pain of abandonment, jealousy, low self-worth, abuse, and so on. You'll do this even though you try to stow away your suitcase and its contents in your subconscious mind. You see, eventually, that the subconscious mind will overflow. Your karma will leak into your life as thoughts, behaviors, emotions, and experiences that you attract or manifest.

Your luggage is not meant to remain unopened and overstuffed.

You can push aside memories of the past and vow never to think about the things that happened that made you feel hurt or angry— but that sort of repression will not work. In your lifetime on earth, you're meant to deal with the pain of the past. You are meant to go through the contents of your karmic suitcase and release the emotions that you feel when reflecting on what has happened to you and what actions you have taken. Otherwise, you will constantly be dealing with your karma's effects on your life, finding yourself in painful situations again and again despite your best efforts to avoid them.

Ideally, you will master your karma so that you will carry very little bad karma with you when you die. Then you won't have much work to do to resolve it in your next incarnation. You will be traveling lightly.

How do you do this? You create good karma through being loving and compassionate, which resolves bad karma and heals wounds of the past. Do not overstuff your luggage by being vindictive, resentful, jealous, or mean—or by mistreating yourself. Yes, you can create bad karma by being cruel to yourself. It's not healthy to tell yourself, "I'm no good, I don't deserve love, I'm damaged goods," and so on. Be loving to yourself always, no matter what. Creating good karma and not bad karma starts there, with how you treat yourself. Being good to yourself helps you avoid creating bad karma with others.

Resolving your karma will rid it of its strong negative emotional imprint. You will still have the memory, but you'll also have the memory of the positive karma you created. After a woman gives birth, she soon forgets how much pain she was in—she can't recall the sensation although she does remember that she was in pain, and may even laugh about it in retrospect. What she remembers most is the joy of holding her baby for the first time. When you resolve bad karma, you will feel grateful for what you learned as a result of a difficult situation. You will see how much you've grown and how far you have come as a result of courageously facing your karma and achieving mastery over it.

The Three Karmic Debts of All Relationships and How Karma Gets Created

All of us have karmic debts. They take different forms, but basically there are three of them: karma carried over from previous lives, karma brought into our lives by others, and karma we create ourselves. You've read about how we carry over karma, but let's go a little deeper into how karma gets created.

Again, when you reincarnate, you choose to be born into a family, situation, and community where you are most likely to have to face your particular karma, because this will give you an opportunity to resolve it. You are here to pay your karmic debts. But how do they get started?

First, you must understand that there is good karma and there is bad karma. Good karma is the result of actions that are founded in love. Sometimes, these are acts of self-sacrifice. A mother who stays up all night to care for her sick child is performing a loving act that creates good karma. Our friend Lisa has a beautiful young son who was diagnosed with cancer, and Lisa spends countless hours at the hospital with her son. When I, Carmen, was five years old, I spent six months in the hospital with asthma, and my mother, Sanda, rarely left my side. I remember even now that my mother would sing to me and make dolls for me out of scraps of fabric. Such acts of maternal love create admirable karma, though you don't have to be a mother to perform them.

In fact, to give lovingly to any human being nurtures the soul—at least, if that soul accepts one's loving actions. When a person is thoughtless, selfish, or cruel, the giver creates good karma but also receives the bad karma created by the ungrateful recipient of their good deeds. Everyone needs to be more careful of to whom they give lovingly!

When it comes to the two of us, as mother and daughter, choosing to end relationships with those who turn uncaring and disrespectful is a karmic issue both of us have yet to master—but we are getting better at it! What we are good at is creating good karma as much as possible. When positive karma is created it removes some of the clutter from the proverbial karmic suitcase.

When we talk about resolving or healing karma, we mean resolving or healing *bad* karma—the karma that is created through selfishness, greed, anger, and fear. The only way to heal this bad karma is through love—through acting in love and thereby creating good karma. This is much easier to do when we learn our karmic lessons.

Karmic Lessons

Relationships are the classrooms for our karmic lessons. We are challenged to be loving toward everyone we interact with—not just those we love but those we work with, live with, and encounter in our daily activities. Acting in a loving way, and creating good karma, goes along with learning karmic lessons about how to be caring and sensitive, how to sacrifice for others, and so on.

On the other side, your soul is well aware that relationships are the primary classroom for karmic revolution. All of us choose the circumstances we are born into as carefully as we would choose the university we wish to attend. If one school is particularly strong in a field of study you are interested in, you will enroll there rather than in a school that is better for a different field of study. Instead of devoting yourself to learning about sociology, computer science, or musical theory, however, you choose to study trust, low self-worth, abandonment, and other karmic issues you have trouble with.

The word *relationship* comes from a Latin root meaning "restore." All relationships are meant to restore people back to their natural state of joy and inner peace. Learn your lessons and you will get there! And maybe you will earn your master's degree in karma, too, if you work hard enough.

You see, karma is at the root of all the relationship struggles that make marriages, friendships, and family relationships complicated and cause us pain. Mastering it frees us from undue suffering in our relationships. Every relationship offers us opportunities to grow, to heal our emotional wounds, to resolve our karma, and to learn our lessons. If we accept that and choose to learn our lessons quickly rather than avoid them, we are less likely to be frustrated, hurt, and betrayed.

There's a line in the movie *As Good As It Gets* when Jack Nicholson's character says to the woman he loves, "You make me want to be a better man." A healthy relationship should inspire such a goal! If you stay in a relationship, devoted to strengthening it and making your partner happy even as you are devoted to taking care of your own emotional needs, you will become a better person and a more loving partner. That's how relationships are supposed to work.

The neighbor, friend, relative, or romantic partner who is upsetting you with his behavior is your potential teacher and may participate with you in healing old, bad karma that is weighing you down. Does your teacher make you want to scream at times? Well, didn't your best teacher in school frustrate you sometimes only to push you past your stubbornness and resistance so that you could learn what was difficult for you to grasp?

When someone frustrates you, you may even have made a soul contract with that individual when you both were souls in the Spirit realm, deciding what to learn in your next lifetimes. On the other side, one soul might say to another, "I'd like to work on trust in the next lifetime, because I was untrustworthy and betrayed my friends in my last life on earth." And the other soul might say, "You know, I need to work on trust, too. How about if I enter your life and betray you so you can better understand this karmic issue? Or you can betray me and I'll be the one who has to learn to forgive and start to trust again. Which would you prefer?"

From the perspective of life on earth, where we do everything possible to avoid discomfort and pain, such an exchange seems impossible, but our perspectives are very different on the other side. We want to sacrifice to evolve, unlike on earth. On the other side, we are aware that we get to choose to be both student and teacher in the classroom of life. That way, everyone will have opportunities to learn karmic lessons. We pick our courses, teachers, and study partners—and eagerly look forward to when the school bell rings and we return to earth.

Here on earth, memories of soul contracts remain hidden in the subconscious mind, but you will indeed meet up with the souls you made the contracts with, and others who can help you resolve your karmic issue. If you're willing to learn your lessons and resolve your karma, even if the other person you're involved with is not willing to do so, you can use the relationship for healing and growth.

Let's say you have a falling-out with a friend. She may never get past her anger at you, but you can choose to forgive her and feel love and compassion when you think of her. In this way, you can resolve your bad karma without holding on to resentment, anger, and grief about the loss of a friendship.

When Karma Begins to Hurt

Does your relationship with someone feel as if you're in a graduate-level class in patience and forgiveness that you're unprepared for? Relationships should be challenging at times because they're meant to make you face your karma, but they should mostly be nurturing, fulfilling, and supportive for you. Love shouldn't hurt or make you feel inadequate or inferior! A romantic partnership or family relationship shouldn't wear you down so much that you're depressed and pessimistic all the time.

If you remain in a relationship and do your best to face your karma and the strong negative emotions you have around issues such as trust and betrayal, generosity and stinginess, nurturing and withholding love, and so on, you can improve your relationships and derive much joy from them. But you also have to take care of yourself. You have many lifetimes in which to learn your karmic lessons and heal bad karma. Don't put up with abuse. Be loving toward yourself. Sometimes, a relationship is too toxic and dangerous for you to remain in it. We'll talk more about that later in the book. For now, just know that you have to be aware of how much challenge you can handle—don't push yourself so hard that you're actually in danger or developing depression.

I, Carmen, remember that my father, Victor, used to say, "The star that cries the most shines the most." It can be very difficult to deal with karma in your relationships because it can cause you much pain, but you will shine brighter. You will actually have a lighter spirit that's less encumbered by karma—a brighter spirit that is more radiant. You're a being of light, and you don't want to be weighed down by the heavy, dark energy of bad karma from the past. And you certainly don't want to put more of it in your suitcase!

So let's take a look at how you accumulated the karma you have now and what your patterns are.

2

BECOMING YOUR OWN BEST FRIEND AND EVEN A QUEEN DIVA

(And Why That Can Liberate the People You Love)

The purpose of our lives is to bridge what we deserve with what we receive.

—ALEXANDRA HARRA

Each of us was born into this world shining with the light of our own inner being. But as the months and years passed, our brilliance dimmed. We forgot our true nature as spiritual beings that are always connected with the divine force that is God. And in forgetting our true nature, we forgot our beauty and our lovability.

We all deserve unconditional love. And the purpose of our lives is to bridge what we deserve with what we receive. In receiving this kind of love, we must also strive to love others unconditionally rather than only if they please us or give us what we want. Love is the foundation of positive, healing relationships, and love begins inside—with ourselves.

Unconditional love doesn't mean accepting disrespectful or abusive behavior. It means choosing to acknowledge the true self—the soul—in others and yourself. It is seeing the entirety of someone, both their strengths and weaknesses, and appreciating them wholly. Profound awareness lies in understanding a person's totality. Acknowledging who you truly are, and loving yourself unconditionally, is what allows you to break free of the ego's habit of focusing on all the problems in your life, seeing yourself as flawed and unlovable, or blaming others for your feelings and circumstances.

When you experience your true self, you're able to look beyond others' egos and your own. You peer into the radiant light of the soul. You accept people as *they* are, because you accept yourself as *you* are. This diminishes your frustrations about trying to "change" someone because you feel they ought to change. Your perception shifts, and your negative emotions melt away. You're able to extend unyielding compassion to yourself and others. You recognize that we're all souls on a journey, trying to achieve healing, love, and connection with others, and that the ego causes us to inflict suffering on ourselves—suffering that is completely unnecessary.

It isn't always easy to love yourself. Most of us store internalized messages about how we're inadequate in some way. Whether we are unhappy with our physical self, feel inadequate in our career, or blame ourselves for mistakes of the past, we all subconsciously sabotage our self-love. Society teaches us that we must strive to be better, yet it seldom teaches us that we should accept ourselves during the process, too.

When you know and love yourself, you become committed to checking your ego, because you know how it can get in the way of your relationships. You no longer automatically react to others with fear and distrust, and you make it a point to see past the behavior of the ego and through to the true self of anyone you encounter. Then you experience completely different kinds of dynamics than you have before. But it all begins with self-love. That doesn't mean you become a total diva who thinks the world revolves around her, but it does mean that you recognize you are an exceptional, brilliant soul worthy of unconditional love and boundless joy (and a *bit* of a diva, too, because that's just fun!).

ALEXANDRA

The Art of Self-Love

Self-love is our saving grace. We often see love as something we should give to others instead of extending to ourselves. Because I am a woman who feels deeply, my first instinct is to care for those around me. That's just who I am, naturally. I give without regret or restraint and rarely expect anything in return. But when I give from the heart, I don't always get love back. I've been burned—badly—by being openhearted.

I know many who are similar to me and see a discouraging pattern—those who have it in their nature to love without limits ironically impede the pathways of self-love. The more they love another, it seems, the less they are able to love themselves. You give and give, get hurt again and again, and start to think there has to be something wrong with you. You wonder if you're unlovable, forgetting that, actually, you can be very lovable and yet be mistreated by other people because of their own unhealed karma. You mistakenly take the burden of not receiving enough love upon yourself.

Having recently escaped a five-year relationship, I found my love levels dangerously low. My adoring energy had been exhausted on another person and now I, newly single, was left unknowing how to rebuild that force within me . . . until a stranger gave me the answer.

It was New Year's Eve and I was at a party, when a man standing next to me casually asked what I did for a living. I told him I managed my mom's psychology business, to which he replied, "Do you know there's one answer to your clients' problems? It's simple: have a love affair with yourself. But don't tell them that, or you won't have a business!" He chuckled and wandered off.

I stood there for a moment thinking, *Okay, that's not what a man typically says to me at a party*. The incident had a strange quality that made me turn it over in my mind as I stood there, champagne glass in hand. Committing his words to memory, I took the fleeting encounter as a signal to live out the coming year differently. I resolved to stop dwelling on the pain I'd experienced in my relationship and make this a year in which I practiced the art of self-love.

My journey began with a few simple questions: Had I really lost any love for myself, or had I stubbornly stowed it under a layer of false admiration for another? Could it be that my self-love was just as intact as it was five years ago? Through careful introspection over the coming weeks and months, I would come to find out that there was nothing missing within me. There was nothing wrong with me—and nothing that I didn't deserve. My attitude began to shift as I rediscovered the secret hiding place of my self-love. It was all there, where I had left it, perfect and whole, but shrouded by a veil of self-imposed doubt, which I needed to remove. Healing would mean letting go of the belief that the problem in my relationship had been that there was something wrong with me. In reality, what was wrong was that I wasn't yet confident enough to say, "I deserve better, and there's something better out there for me."

Through daily efforts, I am able to maintain my newfound sense of self-worth. I've found the following simple actions key in reestablishing a profound love of the self:

- *Forgive yourself.* Every one of us makes mistakes—in relationships, finances, personal decisions, and so on. Mistakes can be costly reminders to think before we act, but they are also encompassed by greater lessons. Remembering this can help you forgive yourself for your failures and discern their higher purpose. There's always a lesson. Focus on that. When you forgive yourself for your shortcomings, you can redirect your attention to new efforts that produce new results.
- *Put yourself first.* I'm not talking about narcissism. I'm talking about not putting other people's needs ahead of yours all the time. When you constantly put yourself

second, you set up a pattern and start to settle for second place in more than one area of life. You put your partner ahead of you, your mother ahead of you, your friends ahead of you, and so on. When do you get to be number one? Reevaluate what it means to put yourself first—engaging in *your* interests, pursuing *your* ambitions, and ensuring *your* well-being. Sometimes it's good for everyone if you take a turn leading the pack.

- *Say "I love you"—to you.* Speak it to yourself every morning. I don't care if it sounds weird. It works. Look in a mirror and say, "I love you" in a loud voice. We automatically critique, blame, and fault ourselves for nearly everything, rarely acknowledging the things we do well or those we ought to be proud of. Shower yourself with daily doses of well-deserved appreciation.

- *Recognize your strengths.* Recognizing your strongest traits endows you with deep knowledge of the self, a precious tool you can use to cultivate your best assets. Understand what your shining qualities are and showcase them with beaming confidence. Once you acknowledge your strengths, you can raise your standards in all elements of life because you recognize your worth. The moment you begin to believe that you *deserve* better is the moment you *receive* better.

- *Do something you love each day.* When was the last time you did something you truly loved, just for the joy of it? Ambition is admirable and so is sacrifice, but our lives have become so busy that we often dismiss simple pleasures to take care of business and take care of others.

Whether it's a hobby, talent, or special craft, take thirty minutes out of your day, each day, to practice what nourishes your soul. Everything can wait while you indulge in your beloved self.

- *Cut out negative influences.* Make a list of the people in your life who have no place being there. You know who they are—those who drain you physically, emotionally, or mentally, and who take advantage of you or cause you to stagnate. People who have this effect on you are holding you back from stretching yourself, taking risks, and growing. Trim away these negative influences on you. Yes, many relationships are worth keeping despite their challenges, but there's probably at least one that you ought to let go of, because its potential for bringing you happiness is minimal. It could be an old friend. It could be a client who pays you well. It doesn't matter. Don't hold on to a relationship with someone who makes you feel awful most of the time. Something and someone better will come to you if you let go of the negative friendships.

- *Release love to yourself.* We hoard our abundant love of the self within us, as if waiting to release it to the right person, when in fact we are meant to release it to ourselves. You aren't self-centered if you acknowledge how lovable you are. Allow your self-love to flow freely by eliminating criticisms, insecurities, and doubts. The attention you give to others should not be greater than the attention you show yourself. Why wait for someone else to love you when you can love yourself first?

- *Celebrate your worth.* It's easy to become distracted by potential achievements and neglect past accomplishments. Celebrate your personal triumphs, both big and small, and let every former victory be a fervent reminder that future wins await, too. Don't be afraid to raise your glass to that amazing person who's conquered their every challenge: you. If you keep a journal, don't just write about all that you've accomplished, but also write about all of the things that make you wonderful. Acknowledge your lovable, valuable qualities. Wouldn't you want to be friends with someone like you just because of who you are? If the answer is no, you need to start validating all the things about yourself that are attractive and marvelous.

- *Thrive on creativity.* We are all remarkably creative, but our originality may be stunted by external factors. For example, your job may not allow you to express your true ingenuity. Your imagination allows you to bring your most brilliant ideas to life if you can open the inventive doors inside you. Creativity begins with wonder, imagination, and not censoring yourself. Don't be afraid of impracticality. Don't say, "Oh, I couldn't possibly do that." Why not dream and see if your dream can become a reality? Incorporate your creative tendencies into everyday life, from the way you dress and speak to the way you decorate your home to how you approach life's challenges, like having less money than you would like or trying to find a parking spot when they all seem to be taken (don't get so creative that you get a ticket, though!). Expand your creative potential to reach its peak in time.

Extending too much love to others can leave you lacking in love for yourself. You must walk the fine line of attending to others and tending to yourself. To love yourself also means to know yourself, and not to deny who you are even if you have flaws—and we all do. Know yourself thoroughly to love yourself unconditionally.

Will the Real You Please Stand Up?

Who is the real you? Every person has two identities: the ego and the true self. The ego is concerned with the matters of everyday life while the true self is concerned with the growth of the soul and the resolution of karma. The ego limits us and reminds us of our suffering, while the true self liberates us and helps us transcend our trials. Our job is to love the innocence and purity that lies buried under the piles of karmic baggage that weigh a person down and cause him or her to be selfish or cruel—whether that person is us or someone else. In short, we have to recognize the true self in everyone and not let our own egos, or anyone else's, limit us from loving ourselves and others. The ego will try to tell you that "all people are the same" or "you can never be happy." The real you is grounded in hope and faith in people. The real you is the you underneath your ego—the you who is committed to resolving bad karma, fulfilling your soul's contract, making spiritual progress, and opening your heart to love.

Knowing and loving your true self gives you the ability to acknowledge the true self in others. Unfortunately, if you're like most people, you forgot that you have a true self, and you identify with your ego and your ego identity—as a mother, a son, a business professional, a teacher, and so on. Your true self is concerned with who you are as a spiritual being. You can take on many different jobs or roles in a lifetime, all the while recognizing that your soul reaches much deeper than any of these titles.

In childhood, we are more in touch with the true self because we're still getting used to human existence again after some time away from earth. Before age ten, a child's sense of objective reality is not solid. Children may have trouble distinguishing between their dreams, their imagination, and the physical world of the senses. They may hold on to a belief in the magical creatures depicted in storybooks even after presented with evidence that these creatures do not exist in the same way that their teachers, their teddy bear, and their breakfast cereal exist. They believe in the power of Santa Claus, a jolly man who gives presents to children out of unconditional love, and don't wonder how he is able to enter every child's home and leave gifts in one night.

As they get older and their logical, rational mind develops more, children become increasingly aware of the rules of the physical world and they stop believing in Santa. They become grounded in this world and give up their faith in that which is impossible according to the analytical mind.

Sadly, their faith in the power of unconditional love erodes, too. It is further damaged when they start to be betrayed by others operating from ego. They are teased or bullied by other children, or treated harshly by adults, and learn to associate love with cruelty and insensitivity. They start to become cynical, unless the people around them intervene and teach them to continue to believe in love.

The real you never stopped believing in the power of love—it was merely distracted by the vanities of the physical world. The real you still exists, and you must get to know that person again.

You see, when you are in touch with your true self, and not misled by your ego, it's much easier to have healthy relationships. You consider everyone's needs and make decisions based on what's good for everyone involved, you included. You're clear on what you need, and you are not distracted by what you've been told you ought to strive for—power over other people, lots of money, fame, and so on. Don't listen to the guidance of people around you who tell you that what you really want is something impermanent that won't stand the test of time. What you want and need is long-term fulfillment, deep joy, and true purpose. These are the real treasures of life, achieved by living according to who you really are and what makes your spirit feel uplifted, what makes you feel that you play a valuable role in the world. You feel this truth deep down and mustn't let yourself be told otherwise.

When you operate from love for yourself, you don't feel you need to prove yourself to earn the love of others. You don't turn into a chameleon, changing your viewpoint and behavior every time you are around a different group of people. You know what you want and you live with integrity. So spend some time with yourself, reflecting on the times in your life when you felt the greatest joy, the highest sense of purpose. Did they happen when you were acting on your ego or your true self? Then you will better know who you really are, and you can bring that person into all your relationships.

You: Inseparable from the Whole

You are but one soul in a sea of interconnected souls, but when you recognize that, you won't feel inferior or worthless. On the contrary, when you understand the unity of all that exists in the universe, you comprehend just how valuable you are. Low self-esteem simply doesn't make sense anymore. Why would you not love and cherish the soul that is you? It's the only portion of you that is permanent and will outlive this lifetime.

The experience of self-worth is a gift we can open when we connect with Spirit and understand that we have been laboring under the false idea that God is "out there" or "up there," removed from us. God is present with us and in us in every moment. God is the life force, and God's nature is love. We are part of love. How can we justify rejecting any part of love?

Remembering your true nature as a child of God begins with the conscious decision to reject the old idea that you are undeserving and inadequate. Whatever actions you have taken or choices you have made in the past, you are not "damaged goods." If you were abused, if you did not say "no" because you were confused by your feelings, if you did something ugly, you are not impure. Your soul's pure light is temporarily clouded by bad karma you have created, carried with you, or taken on as a result of interacting with others who have bad karma. Don't mistake this bad karma, which dims your light, as part of you. You are the pure light underneath. You are not your bad karma, which is reversible and erasable. You are your true self, unstained and unmarked by negativity of the past.

If you recognize your self-worth, you will never allow anyone to lessen it. How can you expect to draw love in if you feel no love for yourself? That's like holding up a magnet to a wooden surface—it will not stick. You need to hold it up to another magnet, to something that has the same charge. The people you attract into your life are reflections of what is happening inside you. They are mirrors of your needs and desires and catalysts of your lacks and faults as well. If you have unresolved karma, you'll attract people and situations that mirror or reflect your issues, struggles, and challenges. If you love and value yourself, you will attract people who love and value you, and situations that reflect the beautiful true self you allow to shine.

You may have noticed that when people are too focused on their own pain, perhaps because they're depressed or have low self-worth, they become self-centered. They don't feel supported by others or God. They feel disconnected, and all their attention is on themselves and how they might alleviate their discomfort. They lock themselves within a tiny world of misery. It's not their fault. They can't help obsessing about what they're doing, thinking, and feeling. The irony is that while they may want to please others, they become so worried about how people perceive them, and so emotionally distressed by their own insecurities, that they don't recognize what other people actually feel. Their energy is consumed by their own worries. The depressed person's imbalanced focus on the self can cause suffering for everyone involved with that person.

When you love yourself enough to value your own needs and desires, your relationships improve and become less complicated. You stop being smothering or neglectful, co-dependent or domineering.

When you are upset with how someone else is treating you, it's important to resist the common temptation to focus on what's outside you—someone else's behavior—and instead focus on your own need for healing your karma. Don't judge yourself. We all have bad karma—and bad habits, and human frailties. Just love yourself, know yourself, and work on resolving your karma. It will cause a domino effect on all the connections around you. Then watch your relationships improve.

Affirmations for Increasing Self-Love

Long before the modern world, we chanted our desires to the universe. We repeated "the rain is coming" when there was a drought and "food is plentiful" when the harvest was slow. We used affirmations as hopeful statements to the Divine to give us what we need. Similarly, you can use affirmations as hopeful statements to improve many aspects of your life, including your outlook of yourself.

To increase your self-love, each morning, when you wake up and look in the mirror as you brush your teeth, stop to look into your eyes and affirm the truth that you are an exquisite expression of divine love. Say aloud, "I am a child of God. I am loving and loved. I am worthy of all the joys and riches in the universe. I love being a part of the universal whole that is pure love. Today, I will remember that I am loved. I will express love to myself and others. I am grateful that I am able to experience how wonderful it is to be me with my unique gifts and personality." Then say to yourself, looking deeply into your eyes, "I love you. I love you. I love you." And say, "Thank you, God, for another day in which to experience love!"

Every day that you say this affirmation, you will find yourself believing it just a little more. If you feel resistance when you are saying it, that's okay. After all, we can't be in a gloriously loving mood each day. Take out a journal or notebook instead, sit quietly for a moment, and write down what you are feeling. See if you can identify the emotion or thought that comes up for you. If not, simply write down that you felt resistant to this affirmation. Can you pinpoint why? Pause for a minute to see if any insights come to you. If they do, write them down. If not, come back to your journal or notebook later in the day, perhaps before you go to bed, and return to the memory of saying the affirmation in the morning. What was the nature of your resistance? What can you learn from it?

You may wish to alter the affirmation (or any other affirmation in this book) to feel more comfortable saying it. If the terms *God* and *Spirit* are a problem for you because of experiences you've had with religious teachings, then use a term that works for you, such as *love* or *universal energy* or *life force*. Speak naturally, as if you were speaking to a person in front of you. God has consciousness but does not have an ego that demands we address God in a certain way, contrary to what we've been taught. Spirit simply wants us to feel and express love. Words should not get in the way of the power of love!

Keep in mind that affirmations should be in the present tense so that you are affirming their truths now, in the present moment. If you resist saying, "I am loving," or you are skeptical about being part of a universal whole, then you have two choices: (1) Continue to say the affirmation until you feel it is true for you. (2) Alter the affirmation slightly so that you feel comfortable. For instance, you might say, "I am becoming more loving. I want to be more loving. I am coming to understand that I am part of a universal whole." If you still feel resistance, you may need more help in letting go of the destructive beliefs about yourself and the love that's available to you and within you.

Keep doing the affirmations and you will come to love yourself more. Then it will be easier to face the truth about the actions you have taken and the way you interact and have interacted with others. You will feel the discomfort of guilt, which is an important emotion designed to get us to slow down and address our karma. Guilt helps us change our beliefs and actions so that we are more loving and act in more loving ways. However, you will find it easier not to judge yourself harshly and not to slip back into denial of your actions. You will learn to tolerate the discomfort of self-examination. Self-love—along with trust in the healing force of divine love—will make it easier to remain present with your painful emotions as you do the work of resolving your karma.

Affirmations actually rewire our brains to generate positive thoughts more easily. Much like exercise, saying affirmations aloud raises the level of feel-good hormones in the body and causes the brain to form new neural networks that support positive thoughts. But affirmations alone don't magically change the circumstances of your life. You have to translate thoughts, words, and beliefs into actions in order to see results. If you tell yourself "I'm beautiful," you'll begin to believe it. You'll also begin to act on it. You'll engage in behaviors that reflect your newfound understanding of your beauty. You may take a bit of extra time in the morning to get ready, or perhaps change your look slightly, or begin exercising regularly. Because you're beautiful, you may begin to take better care of yourself. When you believe what you say, you act on it, and carry your affirmation into reality.

Metaphysically, affirmations affect the universal consciousness that is Spirit. When you think them, you change your body's energy field, which affects the energy field that is universal consciousness. And when you speak them, you emit a sound wave that travels through the air and interacts with the delicate dynamic of the universe. Your words reach God. Remember that a thought is an inner activity, while speech has an outward effect. This is why it's so important to speak your positive thoughts. The universal consciousness will respond in kind, so you should be aware of what thoughts and affirmations you are sending out into the energy field that is shared by all. Affirm the very best about yourself and your life. And when you say affirmations, make yourself believe what you are saying—that is the key to affirming speech into reality.

Here are some empowering affirmations for you to use and tailor to your own needs:

> *I have full power over my decisions and trust that Spirit will guide me to make the best decisions.*
> *I am overflowing with joy, vitality, and energy.*
> *My body is healthy. My mind is brilliant. My heart is at peace. My soul is tranquil.*
> *I acknowledge my own self-worth—my confidence is soaring.*
> *I am at peace with all that has happened, is happening, and will happen.*
> *My efforts are being supported by the universe—my dreams manifest into reality before my eyes.*

Don't forget to make the effort to follow through on your intention with positive action. Take care of your body, engage in activities that revitalize you, and heed the voice of your true self, which is in a constant stream with the universal consciousness.

You can also work with therapists, coaches, and healers to break through old patterns of thought and belief. However, do not expect any of these people to resolve your karma for you. Their job is to assist—yours is to do the work.

Knowing and Becoming Your True Self

To get in touch with your true self—and to accept the guidance your soul can have on you—is to shift your awareness away from everyday concerns. Then you can more easily recognize your interconnectedness with all that exists. This shift happens naturally when you meditate, or spend time with pets, or garden, or when you're outdoors in nature appreciating the beauty of the sunrise and sunset, the water, the earth, the stars, the animals, and the trees. Observing the vastness of the sky or the ocean can help you see how small your problems are in comparison. Observing the changes of the seasons—the flowers that blossom at a certain time of year, or the perfect migration and behaviors of the birds and the squirrels—reminds you that you are part of nature's rhythms, too. You remember that sad times will pass, the momentum for building your nest of security will return, and something new will appear at just the right time, when you most need and desire it.

Nature's lessons about life help us step out of the ego's fear and remember what our true self knows—that this too, in time, shall pass. Whenever I, Carmen, am feeling stressed or sad, I love to sit in my backyard in Florida and look at the lush garden filled with mango trees, towering palm trees, pink bougainvillea, and roses in every color. It instantly lifts me up and reminds me that everything has a season, and that neither joys nor sorrows last forever. Truly we should enjoy life as it is today.

When you feel pain, it is especially important to work through it instead of rejecting it. Abiding by your pain instead of dismissing it helps you pass through it that much more quickly and easily. The sooner you learn your lessons, the sooner winter gives way to spring. This works in two ways: first, working through your pain and learning your lessons helps you make peace with what has happened. This allows you to move on, take new actions, and receive new results. Second, understanding your pain and lessons clears your karma and your road ahead. You progress on both physical and metaphysical levels.

The more you internalize and bury your pain, the more it becomes like stagnant water in a river. Allow your pain to flow through you as it comes, filtering out the impurities of your past, carrying the emotional toxins out of you. Express your emotions so that they do not become stuck inside you, embedded in your energy field and your body.

Take a retreat from your everyday worries. Even simply tossing a ball or stick for your dog to chase as you stand in an open field in the sunshine can bring you back to who you really are, and remind you of your connections to a larger whole of vitality and happiness.

Distracting yourself from your thoughts and feelings doesn't mean you avoid them completely. It means you allow them to surface, you ponder them and feel their intensity, and you let them naturally ebb. Dive into your emotions, both positive and negative, as you would into a deep, tranquil sea. That is to experience the totality of life.

Another way to get in touch with your true self and generate self-love is through a self-love board. You can use a poster board, photographs, and a marker—or a computer program for generating a collage of photos and words you can look at several times throughout the day. Create a collage that reflects the qualities that you most love about yourself. You might use words and phrases such as *friend*, *advocate for animals*, or *patient*. You can use images that capture you at your best or that represent how you see yourself. Go through old photographs of yourself to get in touch with what your qualities are, or write a list of qualities before you begin making the board to guide you in choosing words and images. If you type "affirmation board" or "dream board" into a search engine for images, you can get some ideas for how to create one.

Choose words and images that represent who you are as well as who you aspire to be. Perhaps at this point in your life, you aren't very patient, or you don't feel you're a good friend, but you wish to be and are willing to put in the effort required. Illustrating these aspirations on your self-love board will help you recognize that within you there's potential to bring out and increase the power of these qualities in yourself.

Several times a day—maybe each time you sit back down at your desk before you get back to work after a break, or whenever you go to the restroom or go to your front door—take a look at the board. Linger on each image or word and allow your feelings to arise so that you actually feel like a good friend, a patient person, and so on. Connect yourself to the you that you wish to be— the you who is patient or is a good friend, for example. Let that part of your being gently surface. Become the parts you most admire about yourself.

If you have great shame and feel or know you were abused, which can make it very difficult to be self-loving, we urge you to get therapy and reconnect with Spirit to feel your value and let go of any false beliefs that you deserved or invited the abuse. God is an infinite power that can rescue you from those feelings of shame and low self-worth if you ask the divine power to help you recognize how wonderful you are. All of us are wired to reach out to Spirit because Spirit wants us to rely not just on ourselves but on the totality of the loving force of the universe.

CARMEN

Investing in Yourself

I became and remained the breadwinner of my family from a very young age as my music career took off. Everything my loved ones wanted, I gave them, from houses to cars to the finest education. And this constant giving continued throughout my life. How could I deny my family, whom I loved so dearly, when I could work extra hard and give them what they wanted? But as the years passed, and my career shifted, my family trickled away. I was living in America and my sister had left for Europe, my daughters were all grown up, and my parents and husband had passed away. I found myself with no one to please or take care of . . . save myself.

In my eyes, my husband was the most wonderful, handsome, and perfect man alive. But after his passing more than five years ago, there were suddenly more hours in the day. And with my three grown daughters off on their own, I had no laundry to do, no extra bills to pay, and no messes to clean up. I was also no longer a shoulder to cry on or dear confidant for my loved ones. I could work less and have more free time. But the question was: what would I do with it?

I moved to Florida, near the beach, soon after my husband's death. To occupy my newfound leisure time, I meditated on the gently crashing waves and tried to decipher the seagulls' sad songs. It was during one of these sessions that I realized just how much I adored the ocean. Yet I so rarely experienced its splendor, because I had been investing my time in everything and everyone but myself. In fact, I was weary.

My anecdote is the reality of many. When the people you are sacrificing for and giving to disappear, it's disorienting. After all, you've been cooking meals for them, buying things for them, being their sounding board for ideas, listening to them as they talk about their problems. You almost don't know what to do with yourself, as you still hold on to the nudging instinct to care for someone else. Most of us seldom put ourselves in first place.

With so many important people in my life gone, for the first time, I placed myself on the top of my list of priorities. I felt a world of a difference. My self-love and self-worth spiked as I started to attend to my own needs. I had forgotten how much I enjoyed certain activities, and I'd fallen into a habit of pushing them off my to-do list because there were so many other "important" things I had to accomplish.

I felt a change in my relationships, too. The more I invested in myself, the more the people around me began to recognize my true value—the more they saw down to my true self. I was realizing that they loved me for me, even when I wasn't giving to them. How wonderful it felt to have their love even though I wasn't working to win their approval!

How often are you putting aside your own needs and desires for others? Honestly answering these questions will help you recognize the truth of how you invest your time and efforts:

When was the last time I did something I loved?

Whose guidance am I following?

Let's look at each question separately.

Doing what you love. I had forgotten how much I love to sing. Lately, I've been doing that regularly—in the shower, around the house, in my car—just for the sheer joy of it. Alexandra, on the other hand, loves to drive long distances. It's not something I care for, but I can see that it makes her happy, so I encourage her to do it just because it's what Alexandra needs for her own self-nurturing. She is the queen of road trips and traveling up and down the East Coast by car! Practice heartfelt pleasures—you don't need a "reason" to indulge in little things that make you content.

Make note of who or what is guiding you. All of us hold beliefs we may not even be aware of, beliefs that guide us. The more mindful you are of what your automatic thoughts are, the easier it will be to replace the ones that aren't working for you with ones that are. And if you're guided by other people who seem to know what you need better than you do, think about that. Do they really know you better than you know yourself? Their opinions are just that—opinions. Love and trust yourself. Pray or meditate if you have a big decision to make. Let God or Spirit guide you with signs that speak to you through your intuition. Don't talk yourself out of what your heart and soul know is right for you.

Maintain a relationship with God, Spirit, your Higher Power—listen to your inner knowing, which is guided by Spirit, rather than the advice of others, which is guided by bias and personal opinion. If you don't pray, try it. Ask God to help you know what to do, and sit quietly, awaiting an answer. An image or words may come up for you, or you might suddenly realize you know what to do. If no answer comes, trust that you will get an answer when the timing is right. Waiting can be frustrating, but the Divine knows more than we do about when to give us clear answers. Sometimes, we have to learn the value of praying and waiting so that we can discover the value of a relationship with God—and the value of patience.

You can begin to guide yourself based on your inner knowing when you have discovered your true needs. No two people have the exact same needs. Establish what's most important for you to gain, have, and keep in your life—what you truly need as opposed to what you simply want. When you know your needs, you can begin to understand what route you must take in order to achieve them.

The book of Ecclesiastes says there is "a time to scatter stones and a time to gather them." Often we forget to retrieve our personal stones after we've scattered them about, and our energies remain dispersed in a thousand different directions. Take time not just to participate in your routine but to suspend it and indulge in your wants and needs. Gather your stones to regain peace. Meditate, spend time with your pets and in nature, journal, sing, dance—do whatever brings you back to your true self. Then you will be ready to draw your attention to your relationship with others and see your role in them more clearly. You can approach your relationships from the seat of your true self once you've cleared your heart and mind of pent-up energy.

3

DEVELOPING PATIENCE AND WISDOM ABOUT TIME

(To Get Time on Your Side, Finally)

Know when to act and when to wait. Timing is
everything, and everything in time.

—ALEXANDRA HARRA

We create bad karma in our relationships because we're impatient and don't understand how time and relationships interact. Instead of focusing on what is happening in the present, we dwell on the past and let it define our experiences today. Sometimes we get so focused on the future that we don't see what's happening right in front of us. It is difficult to remain aware of the present moment when there is so much that seems worth worrying about, planning for, longing for, or regretting. Our minds want to jump forward and backward and here and there when they most need to settle down and be still and silent in the present. As the Serenity Prayer reads, "Living one day at a time; Enjoying one moment at a time; Accepting hardships as the pathway to peace; Taking, as He did, this sinful world as it is, not as I would have it; Trusting that He will make all things right if I surrender to His Will." More often than not we must take the world as it is and trust that the Divine will make all things right.

Our discomfort with facing the present can cause us to struggle with relationships. All relationships change over time, but we often fool ourselves into thinking a relationship has remained the same as it always was. We don't like to see that the other person has pulled away or no longer nurtures us. Or we were so convinced the other person would be who we wanted him to be that we lied to ourselves about who he was—and continue to lie to ourselves about who he is. Sometimes we do grasp that a relationship has changed, and we want it to go back to what it was. We hang in there hoping the relationship will improve, that the past will come around again. Meanwhile, we avoid acknowledging how unhappy we are in the present. This does a great disservice to everyone involved.

It would be nice if our relationship problems solved themselves instantly, but resolving karma within a relationship involves a process. It takes time, patience, and hard work, and it starts with being honest with ourselves about what is happening in the relationship right now.

Worrying about the past or future, or wishing that the good old days would come back or that the future will be better, takes your eyes off what is happening in the present—and you must be in the present in order to begin resolving and mastering your karma. If you want to become a karma queen, it's important to align with the four rules of universal time:

- Universal Time Rule #1: Everything is in flux.
- Universal Time Rule #2: Timing matters, because at any given time, the forces around us support certain activities and not others.
- Universal Time Rule #3: Trying to force matters or pressure people doesn't work.
- Universal Time Rule #4: Impatience calls for exploration.

Let's look at each of these in detail.

Universal Time Rule #1: Everything Is in Flux

Everything is changing at all times, even the rocks and the mountains! We don't think about how life is constantly transforming, but when we forget this is true, we can become attached to situations as they were or as they are. Then we create bad karma because we're impatient and frustrated. In Buddhism, it's said that suffering comes from our attachments to how things are, or were, or might be. As long as we look at our circumstances as bad simply because they aren't what we want them to be right now, we cause ourselves grief. We start thinking that anything less than ideal is bad, and we become obsessed with the idea that things are not as we want them to be. Yet when we understand that change is a part of life, we have an easier time accepting what our relationships and our lives are right now in this moment. If you want to master your karma and become a karma queen, you have to accept that time is in a flux. Anchor yourself in the present and deal with things as they are presently, because they could change for better or worse at any given moment.

The paradox is that we have to start with acceptance before trying to make our situations or relationships better. We can have greater influence over the way our relationships transform if we stop resisting how they are right now. The more we let them be, the more they change in our favor—both because that's the way the universe works and because our mind-set helps us be more accepting of the situation. You can't change the ebb and flow of the ocean—you can only admire it.

All relationships must transform. No relationship stays the same. No person is exactly who he or she was in the past. We see changes most obviously in adolescence (and at menopause, which, unfortunately, often coincides with another family member's adolescence!). But everyone, at any stage of life, can change. We just tend not to notice people changing because they usually aren't changing physically in obvious ways, as a child does. We can be fooled into thinking a good friend is the same person she has always been, but it may be that we're ignoring the changes she's undergoing—or that she's hiding them for fear of being rejected by others.

Maybe you feel left behind because someone you love is changing. I, Alexandra, had a best-best-best friend and confidant named Anita. We were the typical girlfriends who finished each other's sentences and indulged in ice cream on Friday nights when the boys didn't return our phone calls. We were inseparable— until we went off to different colleges after high school. Slowly but surely, Anita and I began developing different goals and opinions. Our energy just wasn't syncing the way it used to. Other, new energies got mixed in, and for the first time in our friendship, Anita and I began disagreeing over key matters. I was saddened and hurt that my relationship with Anita couldn't be the same as it had been, but the changes going on in our personal lives and, in turn, in our friendship were both natural and necessary.

So we, two BFFs, eventually parted ways. We could have made the commitment to remain close friends, though our views had changed, but because neither of us felt compelled to do that, the friendship simply faded out. This experience taught me that you can't guarantee you will change at the same rate as someone else. However, Carmen and I believe that if you and the other person are committed to loving each other unconditionally, you can remain close even when you enter different stages of your lives or you seem to be growing away from each other. Whatever choice you make, just be sure to accept that you have changed and so has the other person. Relationships require that we embrace people as they are now—not as they once were or as they might be at some point down the road. And who knows? Maybe in a few years, our lives will be back in sync again and we will pick up where we left off. Stranger things have happened.

You must allow people to change and grow and not stifle their potential. If you keep seeing your younger brother as the baby of the family even as he goes out into the world and becomes successful and a well-respected leader in his community, you're not being fair when you treat him as if he's still not as wise and mature as you are. Maybe he is actually wiser and more successful in many areas of his life, and you're avoiding that difficult truth because it's easier to pretend you are still the smarter older sister. It's natural to tend to keep playing the role we've adopted growing up.

Let yourself transform freely, too. Let others expand in their own ways and at their own pace. You can lovingly speak to them about their transformation, and encourage them or warn them about obstacles you see on the road ahead of them, but don't try to hold them back from their personal growth. Allow them to learn in their own ways and their own time. Love them enough to let them evolve. Love yourself and others as you are right now, understanding that one day you may miss the person you know now after they've undergone certain shifts. There's always room for improvement, yes, and there are always challenges to be met. But remember that change happens. Let your relationships ebb and flow and transform, gently guiding them in the direction you want them to go in, but taking a small step back when you see that they are resistant to your efforts. Leave it in the hands of the Divine.

Because relationships are always changing, communicate regularly with the other person. Talk about everyday aspects, but also talk about what's important to them. Ask questions. People open up when you delve into what matters to them. People generally want to talk, but they may be repressing the urge until a topic that's dear to them is brought up. Keep up with the changes they're undergoing and show strong support. Teenagers often protest when their parents assume they still like the same activities they did a few months before because they want their parents to keep up with where they are now—"Oh, Mom! I don't like going ice skating anymore. That's for little kids!" You can laugh at how silly it seems when a teenager has these expectations, but it makes everyone feel better when their changes are recognized by people around them. It validates their identity. Think about how hurt you are when someone doesn't notice you've made a change in yourself! What if you changed your hair color or lost weight and during your next night out, none of your girlfriends noticed? Everyone wants to be acknowledged for having done the work of improving themselves, and they deserve to be! Everyone wants others to see that they have grown or moved forward in their lives. Compliment people on the changes they've undergone.

And resist the natural urge to act competitively or feel envious when others are doing well. Your time to do well will come, too, and when that happens you wouldn't want anyone disrupting your energy with their jealousy. Live and let live. Encourage them when you see them progressing toward their goals. Doing so creates good karma that eliminates bad karma from the past. No one is today who they were in their past, and all we can do is hope to move in a direction that's right for each of us.

Universal Time Rule #2: Timing Matters

When you communicate with others, be aware of their cycles and their moods. People are better able to handle difficult news or questions when they don't feel rushed or put on the spot in front of others. Nobody likes to be stressed or pressured. In fact,

I, Alexandra, have a bit of a bad habit of cutting people off dramatically whenever they begin to cause me stress (I'm working on it!). I know my friends don't mean any harm when they call me to ask a million questions about the future of their love lives, but there's a time and a place for that, and it's not at 3:00 A.M., or when I'm in the middle of a time-consuming project (like writing this book!). I love myself enough to know I don't deserve to be stressed beyond reasonable bounds by anyone. And I know my mom supports me in my self-care, even though during her drama-karma-queen attacks she will send me 499 theatrical texts back to back. (Carmen does not agree that she overdoes it with the texts, and she feels she must immediately tell her daughter when the cat's gone missing again.) What I have learned is to take a breather and give myself a few minutes to relax before responding to anyone's requests. I know that I will have to return to the difficult conversations later, when I am more grounded and centered (the cat going missing because he's been kidnapped by our neighbor is, indeed, a situation you can't put off for too long). You can't avoid confrontations and expect to maintain good relationships. Have the challenging conversations, but do it in the right timing. Otherwise, you may end up rebutting out of frustration or anger, which can seriously damage your relationship. So hold off on the tough talks until you feel you can adequately hold your tongue and respond in the right way.

If, in any given situation, you're anxious and want an answer right away, stop and think. Can you deal with your anxiety on your own and wait until the person you care about is in a better state to talk about what's important to you? Can you calm yourself down before talking further? It's easier to pay attention to other people's timing when you're not in a panic yourself. The difference between pushing someone's buttons when they're in an already bad mood and waiting to reason with them when they're more receptive is *enormous*. Things can turn ugly quickly when your insecurities or anxieties push someone who's already irritable over the edge. This is why it's crucial to inspect the timing of your conversation. Chances are, you may come across as irritating, even desperate, if you approach someone in the middle of an anxious or "needy" mood swing. You might end up saying hurtful things you don't mean because your words are derived from your pain, not from love or logic.

If the timing for a difficult conversation isn't good but you are agonizing over having to remain silent for a bit, release your elevated emotions by scribbling them furiously in your journal or screaming your words in your bathroom as you shower. You can cry as you take a walk, or recount your frustrations to your cat (if he's back from the neighbor's house)—just don't approach your loved one for a tough conversation in the midst of a compromised mood!

What the two of us find most soothing when we feel anxious is, honestly, praying to Spirit to help us sort it all out—and we usually pray alone but sometimes we'll share a prayer. When we pray, we often close our eyes and imagine how a calm but serious conversation with the person would play out. Envisioning a positive, productive conversation with someone you're in disagreement with is always reassuring, and remembering that God is listening definitely helps, too! I, Alexandra, will also stop for a moment and jot down the points I would like to make when the conversation with the person actually takes place. I highly recommend this, as it readies you to speak smoothly, effectively, and cover all important aspects. I will also start writing about the response I anticipate receiving. Sometimes, when the talk does happen, I receive completely the opposite response, but that's okay—I still feel more prepared than if I had dived into the conversation without premeditated thought. Whether you write out the perfect scenario or envision it in your mind, these techniques can help you become calm and prepare yourself for a positive, realistic conversation with the other person that can provide relief and real answers.

Some people need to have transition time to relax before being ready for a difficult discussion. Don't be so impatient that you wait until five minutes after someone sits down and immediately start talking about your irritation, the problems you're having, or what you want them to do for you. Cycles of the week or month can matter, too—and not just for women who have strong emotional reactions to the hormonal fluctuations of their menstrual cycles! A person might feel more pressured on a Monday, or a Sunday evening, than on a Friday—or more stressed out at the beginning of the month, or in the middle if it coincides with some regular project at work that takes great concentration and effort. Be sensitive to people's timing and your own as well and you'll avoid creating bad karma. Love yourself and others enough to pay attention to the unique timing of everyone involved.

At any given moment, the forces around us support certain activities and not others. When you recognize this, you can work with universal time instead of struggling with it. Respect the natural cycles that affect all of us—the cycles of the seasons (beginning projects when it's cold is more difficult than planning or being introspective) and the cycles of the universe, such as astrology and numerology (whatever you do, be especially careful of your communications when Mercury is in retrograde).

We can't always choose the timing of events that affect us, and our situations may be hard to change until we enter a new cycle where opportunities open up. Even so, we can always be working on healing our karma.

A client named Diana, reluctantly accompanied by her boyfriend, Jason, started coming to see me, Carmen, a few years ago. The pair just wasn't in sync. It wasn't that they didn't love each other, but between Jason's job, which had him moving to a new city every few months, and Diana's anxiety about him being away from home, the relationship had turned sour. I told Diana and her boyfriend that they had a difficult choice to make: either Jason had to make an effort to be home more often and Diana had to work on calming her fears, or they would have to leave each other, because the bad karma was piling up and neither seemed willing to budge. Unfortunately, they both had strong egos at first and resisted doing any of the karmic work they needed to do. However, over a few sessions, they decided they valued the relationship enough to begin the process of reorganizing their karma. The turbulence of clashing egos continued for quite some time, until Jason's job finally stationed him permanently close to home, but at least by then Diana's anxiety had lessened because she'd learned to use some calming techniques such as meditation. The couple's relief might have come earlier, however, had they remained present in the moment right from the start instead of focusing on that far-off time in the future when Jason no longer had to move again and again. It's just easier to deal with situations in the present instead of imagining how you'd like them to be or what they might be in the future.

Universal Time Rule #3: Trying to Force Matters or Pressure People Doesn't Work

If you're impatient, you may end up issuing ultimatums to people. A woman might say to her romantic partner, "If you don't make up your mind in three months about whether to commit to this relationship, I'm out of here!" But ultimatums are for *you*, not other people. And, honestly, ultimatums ultimately end relationships. You can't force people to operate on your timetable. They have their own timing. You can set your boundaries and expectations, but you can't make them change, much less make them change as quickly as you would like them to. Change has to come from their heart—they have to want to put in the necessary effort.

If you feel the need to set a boundary with someone and issue an ultimatum, set one up for yourself as well. Make it a two-way street. Say, "I know you need to take time to make your decision. Just know that if this doesn't happen by such-and-such a time, I may move on," and then follow through on the ultimatum you made for yourself. Don't be angry, hurt, and resentful. Often, people want to change but they don't know how to, or it's too difficult for them because they haven't done it before. Don't assume they're not changing because they don't care about your feelings! Just accept that the other person's timing isn't yours. You might discover that the person changes his or her mind and comes back to you very soon.

Carmen has a friend named Shauna, a consultant who was pressured by a client to perform on-demand consultancy work. Shauna had to tell the client, "I don't feel comfortable working with you under these circumstances. If they change and you decide you can work with me the way I said I need you to work with me, then feel free to call me." Shauna let her client go even though the client owed her money for work she'd done. She let go of her attachment to getting paid and a year later, the client came back, saying she wanted to pick up where they had left off and that she was ready to make the compromise she wasn't willing to make before. People who are committed to change will find their way back into your life.

Our desires about having things unfold our way, on our timing, can make us impatient, but pressuring others to conform to our desires to have them change on our timetable almost never works. When it does, they can become resentful about how they were pushed. And that brings anger into the equation, an element we want to keep out of our relationships by all means. In the time between Shauna parting ways with her client and beginning work with that client again, she examined her emotional issues about confronting people about money and began to develop the habit of speaking up earlier when she first began feeling nervous about how a project was going. This saved her stress because she no longer worked past when her clients' retainers dried up. By not forcing matters or getting angry, she created the opportunity to learn how to better structure her deals with clients—and she gave her client leeway to come around to making a necessary compromise. Now that's being a karma queen, a karmic master!

Universal Time Rule #4:
Impatience Calls for Exploration

Fear is usually what's driving impatience, so when you're impatient, the best thing to do is stop and explore your fear. This includes exploring whether there are any outside pressures pushing you to act (two exercises in one). Do you have to get married to this person, or by a certain time? Are others rushing you to make peace with someone right now, when you need more time to be able to work through your feelings and forgive that person? The following exercise will help you better understand the fear that's driving your impatience. By better understanding your fear, you'll have an easier time letting go of it. Then you'll be more patient and you can focus on the process of transformation.

Exercise: What's Making You Impatient?

When faced with the pressure to make something happen right now, slow down and take the time to answer these questions. You might want to write your answers in a journal so you can go over them again later and see if you have more insights.

- I'm impatient about _____. I want this to happen quickly because _____.

• If it doesn't happen quickly, I'm afraid this will happen: _____.

• I'm also afraid that _____ _____.

• What scares me most right now is _____ _____.

After answering these questions, take a minute or two to focus on your breathing. Just pay attention to how it feels to inhale and exhale. Note whether you feel your pressure elevated from having just explored your fears. If a thought pops up, ignore it and bring your attention back to your breathing. Ask yourself whether any of these fears are actually rational or blown out of proportion by your imagination. Remind yourself that there is a solution to everything, and absolutely nothing is as bad as it seems. Speak to the universe, or a loved one on the other side, and say aloud that you are giving your fears away. A short meditation will help you let go of any fear and tap into the parts of your brain that allow you to be more creative, observant, and optimistic. It will also show you whether your fears are valid or irrational.

When you feel calmer and more ready to address your fears again, revisit the preceding questions and study your answers. Do you feel you might answer differently now? Can you see how you are attached to people behaving a certain way, at a certain time, and how that attachment is making you feel fearful or frustrated?

Then fill in the following:

- If I waited and let this situation unfold naturally, there's a possibility that the following positive outcome might develop: _____
  _____.

- If I take some more time before acting, and practice patience, the following might happen: _____
  _____.

Take time to let the answers come to you. Then affirm the following:

I trust in universal timing. Everything happens in perfect timing. The universe is working on my behalf to bring me everything I desire.

Say the affirmation several times, until you feel yourself believing it.

Too often, we focus on getting others to change when that's usually impossible to achieve. The next time you're impatient with someone who isn't doing what you want him or her to do, use the following exercise, the Impatience Cure.

Exercise: The Impatience Cure

When you're feeling impatient with someone, complete the following statements:

I'm impatient with _____ because he or she is doing this, _____
_____, and not doing this,
_____
_____.

I wish this person would _____
_____.

If this person would just do what I desire, right now, then I would experience _____
_____.

If this person doesn't do what I desire soon, it'll be a problem because _____
_____.

Now take a look at your last two statements. Allow yourself to reread them until you feel a strong emotion arise in you. Then close your eyes and breathe deeply and slowly as you feel the sensation of anger or fear. If you feel your muscles tightening and your breath becoming shallow and quick, just keep trying to breathe deeply and slowly. Don't let yourself create new thoughts. Just focus on what you are feeling. Keep breathing slowly until the feeling subsides. You may find you have to cry first. When you are ready, take a deep breath, filling your lungs while thinking to yourself, *Cleanse.* As you exhale, think, *Release.* Wait a moment and repeat this breath, cleansing your energy field and releasing any vestiges of the difficult emotion. Repeat this cleansing and releasing until you feel calm and centered.

Now, look at the last statement. Note what it was that you feared you would experience. Answer the following questions:

Why do I believe I will have this experience? _____
_____.

Then ask yourself:

What would I like to experience? _____
_____.

Is it possible to have a different experience? _____
_____.

What could *I* do to experience what I'd like to experience? _____
_____.

Give yourself plenty of time to ponder this last question. It isn't until you let go of your fear that you can access your creativity and your subconscious mind's ability to provide clarity and answers to any challenges you face. You already know everything you need to know in order to resolve any problem. The key is to break down the wall of fear so that the answers become visible to you.

In any given situation, we will be faced with limitations as to how much we can do to turn things in our favor. The more we understand what we can and cannot do, the more our solutions become clear to us and we can act to our advantage.

When you complete the Impatience Cure exercise, schedule into your planner the first step toward doing what you need to do to experience what you would like to experience. For example, maybe you wrote, "I need to focus on doing more activities that make me feel happy, like meeting a friend and walking around the art museum." Make that appointment today, and keep it!

Often, we think we have to do things with others to enjoy those particular activities. If you want to try a new restaurant, see a movie or play, or do anything else you wouldn't dream of doing without a friend, challenge yourself to do it by yourself rather than waiting for someone to come with you. In this way, you will learn to feel comfortable meeting your own emotional needs without depending on someone else to help you meet them.

Maybe you'll even make a new friend on your way to the movies! By pushing yourself out of your comfort zone and becoming more independent, you will feel less impatient and frustrated, less dependent on others (and, therefore, less disappointed by them), and be more pleasant company when you do find someone who wants to participate in an activity with you.

Do the What's Making You Impatient? exercise or the Impatience Cure exercise, or both, whenever you feel impatient. You might want to record your answers in a journal and come back to reread them. Look for evidence that the situations you're fearful about aren't necessarily going to happen. Write about your feelings and insights as you look back at what your thoughts were when you were being impatient.

Things do not always happen when you want them to. They happen when the Divine allows them to. Everything you want, you will have, but not in your own time—and not necessarily in the form you envision. Instead of fussing and fretting, sit back and relax in full faith, knowing that it's only a matter of time before the universal flow of time returns to fill your desires. And the truth is that the person you wish to be with may not be meant to be with you. You may think, "But I can't be happy without him!" Try to understand that the Divine may have something better for you in mind. This is why it's important to check in with yourself and with God when it comes to relationships. You can't know everything about another person—you don't have the insight to know whether that person can give you what you want. Just trust that whoever was removed from your life was removed for a reason toward your greater good.

Envisioning Better Relationships

Now that we've said that relationships require living in the moment, we're going to contradict ourselves! You also have to have a vision for what you and the people you're in relationships with could create together.

The word *vision* comes from the Latin *visionem*, meaning "wisdom." Having a vision is having the wisdom to see past certain events in expectation of a greater outcome. Growing up in communist Romania, I, Carmen, dreamed of coming to America with a tenacity and fervor that might scare most people. My personal ambition had been conceived from a very young age, and I remained loyal to my aim throughout the years, allowing it to guide me through the necessary steps to help it come true. I sewed hope into the very fibers of my being, so that my dream became inseparable from who I was. That hope kept the vision alive. I came to realize that all visions are the result of three elements: creativity, action, and perseverance. A vision for your relationship should incorporate all three.

CREATE A BIGGER VISION FOR YOUR RELATIONSHIP

We tend to limit our ideas about who we can be, which limits our relationships and keeps us settling for the lowest level of our potential. Form a clear, detailed picture of what the bigger version of your life looks like, one in which you've already attained your greatest goals and fulfilled your deepest desires. Then paint a mental image of how this richer, fuller life will impact how you will interact with people you're in relationships with—your romantic partner, your parent, your business partner, and so on. What would the relationship be in this vision?

Become clear on your objectives and discuss them with your partner. The vision should be shared. Which details of your vision are shared by your partner and which are not?

TAKE ACTION

Schedule times to talk with those you care about and follow through. Ask for help if you need it. Don't be afraid of getting counseling or mediation. If you feel it will help, go for it. And if you or the other person are concerned about whether the mediator will take one person's side, then both of you should be mindful of any signs that this isn't the person to help the two of you.

Never, ever give up. Simply having a vision does not fulfill it; you must work to materialize your dream. You will experience bumps along the road and people who will try to keep you from succeeding, but you mustn't allow yourself to be intimidated. Remember that you are on a mission to achieve something incredible, and it'll take a lot to stop you.

KEEP YOUR VISION IN YOUR MIND TO INSPIRE
YOU TO PERSEVERE THROUGH DIFFICULTIES

Don't allow yourself to become distracted or deterred from making your vision a reality. If you want to have better communication with your partner so you both feel supported in expressing your needs and getting to explore hidden talents, make a point of checking in with each other. Date night should be about romance, but you also have to have time with your romantic partner to talk about whether you both feel you're reaching your goals. Is he taking more time to play his guitar? Are you working on your assertiveness? Are you both feeling intimately connected and enjoying sex together? Obviously, this last one relates only to sexual partnerships, but of course you want to check in with friends, family members, and creative partners also to be sure your relationship is what you want it to be. Support each other in achieving your long-term vision, which means both of you feeling fulfilled and happy within the relationship as well as with each other. Keep the vision in your head, and if you find yourself not being in sync with the vision, correct your course. Perseverance will keep you on track to creating the relationship you long to experience.

Karmic Lessons to Reflect Upon

Never repeat old mistakes that perpetuate bad karma. Granted, this is easier said than done because we must understand what our mistakes were in the first place. To master karma is to engage in a personal evolution and persistently move forward. Learn from your mistakes and be careful about putting yourself back into situations that will be too challenging. If you know a certain type of person triggers old behavior patterns that make you angry, secretive, and vindictive, don't get involved with that person. And you'll know right after meeting someone new whether they'll be a trigger for those tendencies. We often meet people who are "testers," put in our lives by the Divine to test our progress and see whether we've really changed. You can't cheat the all-knowing universe, so make sure you really stick to your changes, or the Divine will know! There will be plenty of opportunities in life to work through the old karma and resolve it at last without you seeking out the craziest, most difficult people to help you learn your karmic lessons. We need normal people in the mix, too. The idea is to resolve bad karma, not to become so frustrated by others that you make mistakes and create more of it.

Learning about karmic cycles can help tremendously as you plan your future with your partner or family and as you try to explore the karmic lessons to be learned. In the next chapter, you'll discover how to use the ancient art of numerology to help you work with the cycles of time and understand how karma is affecting your relationships.

4

WORKING WITH KARMIC CYCLES

(So You Don't Work against Them and Nearly Lose Your Mind!)

*Numbers are the rhythm of the spirit and
the language of the universe.*

—DR. CARMEN HARRA

As Ecclesiastes says, "There is a time for everything, and a season for every activity under the heavens." We are all interconnected with each other and the rhythms of the universe, and we cannot recalculate the perfect timing of the Divine. It's already predestined. There's a time for peace and a time for discord or conflict, which are also part of a healthy relationship. There are times that are best for beginning a relationship and times that are best for ending one. There are times to move forward with your partner and times to stay still and reflect. The rhythms of the universe that affect relationships are called karmic cycles. If you learn to abide by them, you'll learn to master your karma.

You can determine karmic cycles by looking at numbers—yes, numbers. Our physical world is based on numbers. In fact, if you take a closer look at daily life, you'll notice that its every element is numerically grounded: the times we have to wake up, go to work, be at an appointment, come home. How much things cost, how much we earn, and the entire concept of money. Street numbers, phone numbers, ID numbers, ages, and so on. Even when it comes to our health, we look at numbers—a standard blood test will count the number of healthy blood cells, triglycerides, and hormones. And of course, there's the number that's most important to each of us—our birth date. It's no coincidence that you entered this world at an exact second, minute, hour, day, month, and year. This combination of numbers is as unique to you as your thumbprint, and spells out your life in copious detail (probably even more than you'd like to know). The ancient science of decoding the numerological codes that hold such sensitive, personal information is called *numerology*.

Numerology has existed for thousands of years, dating back to Babylonia and Pythagoras. It has ancient roots in nearly every religion—Kabbalah, for example, is largely based on numerology. Certainly it has been active in human function before calculators, watches, or Facebook (which can also tell you the exact second a couple splits up or gets back together).

Two important numbers or codes can help you understand how your karma affects you in your relationships—your *destiny code* and your *personal year*. Your destiny code is set at the time of your birth and does not change. Your personal year changes each year on your birthday and moves in cycles of 1 to 9. And your relationship with another person will be profoundly affected by that person's numbers or codes, as well as the date and time at which you meet, become committed to each other, or marry. Numerology will tell you if you and a romantic partner are meant to be together, for how long, and whether the two of you know each other from a previous lifetime or have only begun creating karma together in this lifetime. You always have free will when it comes to creating and resolving karma, but working with the numbers means working with the flow of universal energy and not trying to work against it (you can't hope to go against the universe and win!). If you have ever tried to walk against a strong headwind, you know what a workout it can be. This is what it feels like working on a relationship in the wrong timing, or working on one that's not meant to be according to the numbers. Make your life easier by becoming familiar with your codes so you can start to understand the many interwoven numbers that indicate the energies that affect you, your friends, family, and relationships.

Numerology 101: The Energies of Numbers

The world we live in is composed of energy that can be translated into numbers, which are the language of the universe. Every date and name can be reduced to a single-digit number, and each number 1 through 9 carries a certain energy. All numbers are calculated by adding up single digits, and if that gives you a two-digit number, you add those two digits together, and if *that* still gives you a two-digit number, you add the digits yet again until you get one number. Thus, the number 97 would be reduced to 9 plus 7, making 16, and you would add 1 plus 6 to get 7—now you have passed the numerology math exam! I, Carmen, discussed numerology at length in my book *Decoding Your Destiny*, including how life path numbers match up to calculate compatibility in couples. The following is a brief explanation of the numbers and the energies they carry. (If this seems abstract, trust us—the energies associated with numbers will make more sense as you learn more about destiny codes, personal years, and karmic cycles in this chapter!)

1: Carries the energy of beginnings and planting seeds. Choose dates and personal years of 1 to marry or renew vows, because the energy supports a lasting relationship. If you break up with someone in a Year 1, or have a falling out, you are likely to be able to resolve it.

2: Carries the energy of gestation, planning, and healing, so a Year 2 is a good time for making peace with the people in your life. In a Year 2, you get ideas for the future but they are not ready to come to fruition. It's an ideal time for developing strategies.

3: Carries the energy of building and growth. It is not the best time for starting relationships but for fostering and nurturing the ones you have. You can build emotional intimacy and trust in this year. This is also a year to put your creative juices to work.

4: Carries the energy of karma and responsibility. It's a year for facing karma from the past and working through it. Unexpected people often come into your life in a Year 4, because you have a karmic relationship with them. In a karmic relationship, there's an intensity that comes from the experiences the people share going back to previous lifetimes. Karma can be quite a powerful force!

It's easiest to get to the root of conflicts in a karmic year like the Year 4 (Year 8 is the other karmic year). You can see what you have to work on and how your choices led to your current situation. A Year 4 is ideal to stabilize finances, which is something to consider when you're looking to get involved in a relationship that has a financial aspect to it, such as a marriage or business partnership.

5: Carries the energy of freedom and new experiences. This is a breakthrough year when problems resolve and you find you're (sometimes suddenly) no longer caught up in old issues and conflicts. Energies flow more freely. A Year 5 is a great year for pregnancy, moving to a new location, and breaking through blockages of any type.

6: Carries the energy of love and joy. You can straighten out any issues between you and others more easily in a Year 6. You're likely to meet someone who will become a very close friend, or a romantic partner, when influenced by the energy of 6. You can also more easily heal wounds and make peace within your family or circle of friends. It is the time to have fun, take it easy, and have reunions. Praise Spirit when you enter a Year 6!

7: Carries the energy of introspection and reflection. This

is not a time to make major changes in relationships but to ponder on them more deeply. It's a time for spiritual growth and recognizing that we're each on our own spiritual journey and must carry out a unique mission. Discover yours in a Year 7.

8: Carries the energy of power and abundance. A Year 8 is like harvest time. If you planted good seeds and tended them well, your relationship will give you great nourishment this year. If you planted poor seeds and didn't put effort in your relationship, you will experience the consequences of your choices. Year 8 is a time for recognition, for being appreciated and rewarded as well as a time for financial progress and the perfect moment to resolve all karmic issues.

9: Carries the energy of completion. If you break up with someone while being influenced by the energy of the number 9, you will have closure rather than become stuck in an on-again/off-again dynamic. But this is certainly not the year to begin anything new! Don't even begin a new game of Sudoku! (We joke, of course.) Things in your life will come to an end, often abruptly, and you will feel the energy of new beginnings in the air as the karmic cycle comes to a close and the Year 1 approaches once more.

There are two other numbers, called master numbers, that carry energy, too: 11 and 22. Eleven is the most elevated of the spiritual numbers, carrying the energy of intuition, illumination, and enlightenment. Twenty-two is the most powerful number, often called the "master builder" number because it denotes success and power without limits. I, Alexandra, am sure I would have found my attempts at world domination much less tedious had my destiny code been a 22.

All codes, or numbers, are calculated by adding numbers and reducing them to a single digit, except when you get a master number of 11 or 22. Simple enough, yes? Now let's move on to the fun stuff.

Your Birth Code and Your Personal Year

All your relationships start with *you*, so it's important to know your destiny code and personal year before evaluating the potential of any relationship. A birth code, or destiny code, sets a certain life path and ensures that the person will have to deal with a specific karma throughout their life. When two individuals' birth codes are compared, much can be learned about what will (or will not) unfold in their relationship. Understand the tension between the energy of your and your partner's birth codes and you will better understand what drew you together and the karma that could potentially tear you apart. These codes can reveal compatibility, durability, fate, and depth in any given relationship.

So let's say you were born May 5, 1984. You would use a 5 (for May) and add $5 + 1 + 9 + 8 + 4$, which comes to 32. Then you add the 3 and 2 to bring the number down to the single digit 5. Your destiny code, or birth code, would be 5.

Looking at the following list of the energies of numbers, you can see how these energies would affect a person's temperament, character, and destiny:

Birth Code 1: A person who is born to lead, who tends to be the first to start something or begin a relationship, reaching out to others. Ones tend to be people of action and are often quite driven, but they can be overly independent, preferring to be alone rather than with their partner.

Birth Code 2: A person who is diplomatic and good at conforming to the needs of others, who can struggle to take the lead and be the star of the show but tunes in to others well. Twos tend to be very sensitive and emotional and good at healing rifts, carrying a nurturing energy.

Birth Code 3: A person who works hard at building and creating something new, who is drawn to self-expression. Threes often are innovators or artists who aren't happy unless they are productive and working creatively.

Birth Code 4: A person who draws upon the past to move forward into the future, who values memory and history and is devoted to learning his lessons. Fours are often very grounded people, and you will see their stability and respect for strong foundations reflected in their wealth and careers as well as their commitment to relationships.

Birth Code 5: A person who must have freedom and travel—whether it's actual travel or exploring the world of imagination and ideas so as to expand one's mind and soul. They can't be happy if they are pinned down, so in a committed relationship, they must have their time and space to grow and evolve the undeveloped aspects of themselves. They have to have alone time, and relationships with friends outside marriage or romantic partnerships, and also need space for creative interests outside their main creative partnership. They may be great collaborators, but only if they have the freedom to express themselves on their own, too.

Birth Code 6: A person who is warmhearted and loves to be with others, helping them out and being a social butterfly. A six needs to be at the center of the party, the family, the group of friends, or the community. It's interesting that some people who tend to be the "hub" through which people connect with each other are said to be "six degrees of separation from everyone else in the world." That's a six.

Birth Code 7: A person who is destined to be introspective and reflective, to make serious spiritual progress in this lifetime. Sevens are often wise beyond their years when in youth, and elders and others often look to them for advice even when the sevens are still rather young.

Birth Code 8: A person who is destined to achieve and feel comfortable with power, abundance, and even fame and fortune. Eights are goal-driven and motivated, so they often achieve much worldly success because they build on the lessons they have learned and the strength they have acquired, yet they are often artistic and dreamers, too.

Birth Code 9: A person who is completing a cycle and who came into this incarnation to be a visionary or leader that serves humanity. Nines are often very old souls who see the larger picture and don't get bogged down in the small dramas of life.

If you read these descriptions and think, "That's not me at all," ask yourself whether these energies seem to be ones you are resisting. It may be that you came here to learn to own your need to be free like a 5, or a visionary like a 9, but haven't resolved the karma that's holding you back from your destiny. Don't underestimate the power of those numbers to push you into situations and relationships that make it hard to resist accepting your destiny!

Your destiny code interacts with your personal year, which also has an energy corresponding to the numbers 1 through 9. Knowing which personal year you are in can help you understand the experiences you will have in that twelve months between birthdays. Since the universe delegates our time, there are personal years perfect for getting married and personal years in which you shouldn't dream of starting a new relationship unless you're up for a lot of heartache. If you pay attention to what personal year you are beginning, within, or just coming out of, you can decipher exactly what you will need to work on, anticipate, and avoid during the year.

Your personal year begins on your birthday and ends on your

birthday. If your birthday is May 5, then in 2015, as you approach your birthday, you will be coming into a Year 9 ($5 + 5 + 2 + 0 + 1 + 5 = 18$, $1 + 8 = 9$). Nine is a year for endings and tying up loose ends. That would be a good year for you to end a relationship or partnership peacefully and know that you will heal your karma from the relationship more easily than if you were to break up in a Year 4, let's say, which is a karmic year. It's likely you'll have unresolved karma and find yourself interacting with that person again—and not necessarily in a pleasant way. If you were to break up in a Year 9, which carries the energy of ending, the split would be likely to be permanent as you begin a life outside the one you had when you were married or in a close friendship with that person.

Birth codes also reveal the issues you need to work on. If you are an eight and have several eights in your birthdate (for example, if you were born in the eighth month, on the eighth day), you will be strongly affected by the energy of eight. But what about the numbers missing from your code when you look at the day you were born, the month, and the year as well as your single-digit destiny code? If you're missing a particular number in your code, you're likely to have to face issues regarding that number. And if you and your partner are both missing a number, you will certainly face the issues associated with that number together. So, for example, let's say you look at the birthdates and birth codes of yourself and your romantic partner and neither of you has a 7, the number of reflection and acceptance as a person ascends to a higher level of awareness. Your partnership can still be a deep one, in which you help each other develop spiritually, but that destiny may present challenges. What you miss, you must work on—and you may find that circumstances that force you and your partner to reflect or practice awareness or spirituality keep coming up in the relationship. You will have to face the challenge of what is not there and supplement it through your own learning, awareness, and actions.

I, Carmen, have a strong influence of the number 7 in my birth code and 7 is my destiny code, so it makes sense that I've been focused on spiritual matters for most of my life. Virgil, however, did not have a 7 in his code. He was much more practical, pragmatic, and even skeptical about metaphysics at times. But we complemented each other: I taught Virgil the basics of spirituality and helped him develop that part of himself—and over time he began to believe in the Divine, at least halfway. On the other hand, I'm missing a number 4 in my code, the number of stability, grounding, and a "home." Virgil gave me that stability on every level, by being my husband, best friend, wise advisor, and protector, and someone with whom I could build financial security. Yes.

Now let's say that you and your partner share numbers—for example, if you both have a number 3 in your codes, the number of creativity, charisma, and talent, then the lesson of becoming creative comes easily. You would experience creativity strongly, as the energy of 3 would be radiating from both of you. What you have already in your code, you don't need to learn again unless the energies of other numbers are stifling your destiny and pushing you to resolve karma and create relationships with people who challenge you.

Also, if someone's divine code coincides with the *year* the other person was born, it's a karmic relationship (for example, if you're a number 6 and your partner's year adds up to a number 6).

Relationships in Sync with Karmic Cycles

In an ideal world, you and your romantic partner would marry in a personal Year 1 for each of you because that's a year that's conducive to beginning endeavors. You would ideally choose a date that has a code of 1 as well. The more ones in the codes, the stronger the marriage, as the universal time is appropriate for new beginnings.

But since this is far from an ideal world, when you factor in your partner's numerology and cycles, and the dates on which you marry or become official, you will probably end up with some conflicts in energy. That's okay, because these issues will give you both a chance to grow and learn together, so long as you are both willing to work and compromise.

The science of numerology shows us that the "coincidence" of numbers matching is anything but. It teaches us that when you work with cycles instead of against them, everything happens more smoothly. When you are out of sync with them, you have to work much harder to get your relationships back on track.

I, Carmen, had a client named Jennifer who was determined to get married in a year that was a personal Year 9 for her and for her husband as well. Jennifer insisted that if she and her husband-to-be didn't marry now, it would never happen. Her urgency was in large part due to pressure from her mother-in-law, who wanted to see her son married off. Ah, good old external influences! Jennifer and her husband were divorced five months after their wedding date. But they weren't meant to part ways permanently—just until the time for connection came around again.

There came a time when Jennifer's ex-husband wanted her back, but she was very worried. It seemed they had worked through their differences, but she wasn't sure. However, this time, the numbers showed that she and her now ex-husband would be able to retain their commitment to each other. They were both in a Year 6, which is convenient to reconciliation and lasting love. Jennifer and her ex-husband decided to remarry, and this time they finally enjoyed the relationship they had hoped to have the first time around.

It's not that the two of them magically had all their problems erased when they reconciled by chance in a Year 6. If only it were that easy! The point of paying attention to cycles is to know what you're in for. Being too ambitious about working through your issues in a personal year that carries the energy of karmic challenges can lead to unnecessary strife. You can always be working on your relationship with each other, but don't put too much pressure on the partnership by committing to each other in a year in which you're both strongly affected by the energy of endings and not beginnings. Let the right time return, as it always does.

We all have free will, however, and can make whatever choices we like. Just be mindful that your choices are inseparable from the universal time that governs the world. Why work against the universal cycles when you can work with them? In the end, you can work through a relationship even if you are not a numerological match. However, you must work hard to make it happen and you have to believe it will. Determination counts for a lot!

Often, I, Carmen, am asked to predict whether a relationship will work out. I use numerology as one tool, intuition as another, and psychology as still another. Combining these three methods,

I often get a clear sense of when two people have the best opportunity for reconciliation. But because they have free will, the two people may not choose to make the most of this opportunity. I might say, "I can see you and your sister coming together to do a project, and your relationship gets solidified because of it." But if you and your sister decide not to work together, and instead you hold on to your old resentments toward each other, the reconciliation won't happen. A prediction reflects a possibility, not an inevitability. Being intuitive doesn't mean you have a magic wand to force two people suddenly to get along beautifully! If I could do that, I would have resolved the world's problems a long time ago.

Another client, Philip, separated from his wife after nine years of marriage and called me in tears that he wanted her back but was unsure of whether the relationship could work out in the long run. He had many doubts, and the relationship had many bad influences coming from both families. His heart was clearly committed to her and the relationship, and the numbers showed that they had karma to work through. I told Philip to give his wife another chance because his karma needed to be resolved in one way or another, with her or with someone else. With his deep devotion, and willingness to resolve the issues, the relationship might work out despite the outside influences and his wife's personal problems. For both Philip and his wife, the numbers associated with karma were more influential than the numbers associated with harmony and joy. For now, they would work out their karma, until the numbers cycled around to a less troubled time in their partnership.

Our lives go in cycles of nine years, so big emotional commitments to friendships and partnerships may need to wait a long time if you want to avoid conflicts and heartache. If you missed your big chance to reconcile with someone fully, or create a powerful bond together, another chance will come, but you may have to wait several years. Life is like a merry-go-round: you always get another opportunity once the ride comes around. You can make your peace with someone, but your trust in each other may be shaky for years until the wheel of time turns and an opportunity for a truly strong reconciliation returns. If you have agreed to a truce, renew that commitment in a personal Year 1 or 2 for both of you, if you can. Just be patient, for whatever is meant to return into your life will steadily find its way.

Process, Not Timing

While working with—instead of against—karmic cycles supports better relationships, it's important to pay attention to the *process* of resolving karma—not just the timing. Everyone wants relationship problems solved instantly, but healing old hurts, tending to the wounds caused by betrayal and neglect, and creating emotional intimacy to replace trust issues involves a process that should never be neglected. Relationships are the ground on which we heal our karma and become karmic queens, triumphing over the behavior patterns that used to cause us pain again and again. Never stop working on resolving your karma that affects your relationships—even if you break off a relationship. Don't look to numbers to rescue you from the hard work of relationships!

If you experience a breakup, someone will come into your life who will display karmic issues similar to those of the person you split from, and you can work on your issues with them. Try to make sure that this person's karmic issues aren't quite so intense! They may not be if you've worked on your own issues, too. So if you tend to give too much in a relationship, you may meet another needy person you're strongly attracted to, but at least this potential partner is employed, is honest, and won't lean on you for absolutely everything! You're making karmic progress.

Because we're so impatient, we tend to overlook people's flaws when we're desperate to have a romantic partner again—or a best friend to spend time with, or a business partner willing to work hard alongside us. Desperation causes us to accept unfortunate circumstances and allow them into our lives, despite knowing deep down that they are wrong for us. Although I, Carmen, can give people predictions about when something will happen, I know well that impatience leads many people to focus on the timing of an event rather than the process of bringing it about. You will find the right person. You will find a marvelous business partner, best friend, leader for your group, and so on—but not if you're so anxious that you willfully ignore any signs that the person you're considering a relationship with has some serious problems. Then you are going to get involved with the wrong person, despite the universe's warnings!

Again and again, women ask me, "When will I get married?" and they express anxiety because they're nearly thirty or forty and they've gotten it into their heads that they have to be married by a certain age. As an intuitive, I may be able to tell them very specific details about when they will meet someone—I once told a woman that she would meet her man at a St. Patrick's Day party, and sure enough, she did. But it was the *following* St. Patrick's Day, so she had to wait another year (she wasn't too happy about that, but when she finally met her guy she was in heaven). The point was, "Go to the party on St. Patrick's Day and for goodness' sakes, if you see a man who looks like the one I described in our session, don't come home without his phone number!"

You must take the initiative to work with the timing of the universe to make something happen but you must be patient, too. You have to go to that St. Patrick's Day party, of course, but you also have to do the work inside you that will ready you for a long-term, emotionally intimate commitment. Otherwise, you may meet twenty different great men at the party, even St. Patrick himself, but none of the connections will last or work out. That's a sign that you didn't do your inner work. But if you engage the process of resolving your karma and you use all of your relationships as classrooms for learning and letting go of old ideas and habits, you can meet the perfect mate, fall in love instantly, marry quickly, and live together happily for many years. If you've worked on your karma, who says fairy tales can't become reality? There's a delicate balance to be respected that includes patience in the wrong times, action in the right times, constant healing, inner work, and unbound faith in the power of the Divine. This, this is the recipe for fostering potential into actuality.

In fact, in the process of working on your relationships with friends, brothers, sisters, and even neighbors, you start to learn more about yourself and what you need. It's difficult for people in their twenties to know what they want in their romantic relationships and much easier for people in their forties and fifties who have come to know and accept their strengths and weaknesses, and have learned what they want and don't want in a partner. Having a focus on all your relationships in the present rather than some perfect romantic relationship off in the unknown future makes it more likely that you will attract the right person for you and create the relationship you want without constantly struggling. Having realistic, grounded expectations and being ready to compromise certainly doesn't hurt, either.

Remaining focused on the present brings two gifts: patience and wisdom. You're not fretting about when something will happen, and you're also accepting that it will happen in just the right time. You become patient because you get used to being here, in the moment, instead of worrying about the future or hoping that all your relationship problems will get better someday. You're also not caught up in resentment about the past, or longing for a relationship that has ended. Living outside time, in the past or future, disempowers you. It diminishes the authority you have today, right now. The power lies in what you can do this very moment using the tools you have right in front of you. And you can usually do more than you think.

Today, you can work on your relationships and reflect on what is and isn't working. Stick with the process! And remember: slowing down to reflect is key to developing wisdom. The more patient you become, the more often you stop reacting to the world and take time to consider your actions, feelings, and beliefs, the wiser you become. Wisdom isn't reserved for old age. A young person who is habitually reflective may be much wiser than an older person who never looks closely at her choices and behaviors and instead focuses on how other people act. This outward focus contributes to a habit of jumping out of the present time. The person thinks, "I hate that he did that to me!" or "I wish she would change!" or "If only our relationship could be like it used to be—I'm so depressed that it isn't." Thoughts like this contribute nothing positive to the progress of a relationship. Be fully present in your relationships today and you will become wiser over time.

One of my clients wanted to reconcile with her ex-husband, and I, Carmen, predicted he would come back to her in two months. Focused on timing and not process, my client took the prediction far too literally. Her former husband did reach out to her through an e-mail in which he said he would like to talk with her. He was dipping his toe in the water, and she thought he was diving in headfirst. She was expecting him to show up at her door with an armload of roses saying, "I'm so sorry. It was all my fault. Let's try again." This was a woman who had said she had discovered that every man she had been with had the same problem—he didn't give her enough attention (in her opinion). Her expectations were unrealistic and based on the idea that the old pattern would be broken instantly—by someone else's actions. Her attitude was, "Let him do the work!" What she needed to do was focus on the process of changing her own beliefs and resolving her own issues. She needed to ask herself, "Why do I look to men to make me feel valued? Is there another way to meet my emotional needs besides getting involved with men who are in a stage of life where other priorities come first?" She refused to look into *her* pattern. Sadly, her ex-husband remained her ex-husband after they sat and spoke and he realized she had not changed. Patterns must be identified and examined before they can be broken.

CARMEN

Even Karma Queens Can't Escape Karmic Cycles

My father used to say, "My dear Carmen, life is algebra." By this, he meant that life is full of ups and downs, pluses and minuses—and I've come to understand that life is also algebraic in that it is precalculated or predestined. Mathematics adheres to strict rules—two plus two will always equal four, and four minus two will always equal two. There's a certain beauty to the predictability of it. When we break down numerology to the science that it is, we begin to believe in the mathematics of birth, death, and everything in between. There are no coincidences between anniversaries of family deaths and births clustered in a month. That's because the timing of all things is intertwined. And divine timing makes itself visible through synchronicity that just can't be ignored. All you have to do is look at the numbers and pay attention. I guarantee you it's more fun—and much more beneficial—than your former algebra classes.

In my family, November is a big month. All of my major life events have happened in November. Now, many have occurred during my birth month of March, too (my sister, my mother, and I were all born in that month), but November is *the* karmic month in my family. My mom and dad married on November 8, exactly 50 years before my mom's death to the very day. My mom was married to my dad for 43 years (which equals a number 7 when you add the digits), and seven years after losing him, she passed. My stepdaughter who is also named Carmen was born on November 8. And I got married to my husband on November 8. That was *not* planned: Virgil and I had gone to city hall four different times to try to get married. The first time, the computer was down. Then there was a holiday we'd forgotten about—and so it went, on four separate occasions. When we realized we were marrying on November 8, we thought, *How weird!* It was as if fate were forcing us to marry on that date. And a few years later, Alexandra was born—on November 8. Oh, and my other daughter Florina was born on November 4! What's up with all of these November dates? For starters, Carmen and Florina, though not my biological children, were meant to be in my life just as much as Alexandra was! And Virgil's and my families were meant to be intertwined.

As I said, my mother passed on November 8—she died the day of her fiftieth anniversary of marriage to my dad. The number 5 (50 is 5 plus 0) signifies the house of transit of death. Alexandra turned 14 the day my mom died, and that equals a 5, too. Everything is sewn inextricably together because of our karmic ties. More so, my husband's first wife (to my delight) shares my birthday, the same year and all! It's because we were destined to meet in this lifetime. Believe me, synchronicity is no accident, and the deeper we delve into it the more we understand the magic threads of our fate, made evident by recurring numbers.

It gets stranger. Until recently, I didn't even realize something incredible about my mother's anniversary. She was 70 years and 7 months when she passed, and my dad died at 70 years and 7 months. The seven followed them *everywhere.* My mom will have died 14 years ago this November, and next year, we think she might come back in a new incarnation. (I hope Alexandra agrees, as it will have to be through her!)

Major events happen in the same time because the universal energy is productive to change. A lot happens especially in the month of your birthday, because you end an old cycle and begin a new one. Look closely at dates—pay attention to numbers of dates of birth, death, marriage, and other significant events. Study the dates in your life, in your own family, and see what you find. Do you notice some of the mysteries of your life unraveled through the workings of repeating numbers and dates? It's fascinating to discover new patterns you might otherwise miss, helping to put life into a new, karmic perspective.

5

THE ACORN DOESN'T FALL FAR FROM THE TREE

(Even If You Wish It Would So Your Adult Child Would Move Out!)

No family is perfect, but your family is perfect for your karma.

—ALEXANDRA HARRA

CARMEN

The Joys of Family

If I look back at my household ten years ago, I would say it was more a jungle than a home. My husband and I had three daughters; my estranged cousin, Silviu, had moved in with us (although I never did find out how he was related to me); my husband's slew of family members barged in on a daily basis; and seven cats and one dog rounded out the family. Somehow, all of us fit into a typical attached brick house in Queens, New York. Since my late husband was an art dealer, the place resembled an antique museum, with portraits of nude women adorning the walls and enormous bronze statues situated in every corner.

As for our three daughters, Alexandra, the youngest, was sixteen at the time and passing through the worst of her rebellious phase. (Has your child ever crawled catlike into your bedroom in the middle of the night and stolen $120 from your wallet to get a unicorn tattoo on her breast? I didn't think so.) Our daughters Carmen and Florina were twenty-six and twenty-seven, respectively, and although Carmen was already settled down, Florina was still a wild child, to say the least. In fact, she and Alexandra often competed for "queen of crazy."

One argument to top the charts took place late one night as Alexandra was heard bellowing down the stairs at her sister. She was leaning over the banister while Florina, below, was accusing Alexandra of "stealing her man" in less-than-ladylike vocabulary. My husband and I were awoken by their shrieks and yells over this case of twisted love. Apparently, Florina's then-boyfriend, a short, sketchy guy with a motorcycle, tattoos littering his body, and a few misdemeanors under his belt, had come on to Alexandra. Alexandra claims to have steadfastly refused his indecent proposals, but Florina wasn't so convinced. The back-and-forth accusations continued until my husband stepped in. He swore to send them both to Romania if they didn't stop. The yelling ceased immediately, but the sisters didn't speak for days.

I understood both sides. Both Alexandra and Florina felt hurt and betrayed—Florina by the thought that Alexandra would dare flirt with her boyfriend, and Alexandra by the thought that Florina could think that of her. Seeing that my daughters weren't reconciling, I felt it was time to step in. I sat Alexandra and Florina down and asked each of them to tell their version of the story directly to me. I asked each one not to interrupt the other while she was speaking. This would allow one to really listen to the other in a nonargumentative way.

Though at first hesitant, each sister released her frustrations and emotions to me, and confessed that she felt horrible for fighting with each other over some guy. Alexandra understood that she was wrong in not speaking up when Florina's boyfriend had first tried to sweet-talk her, and Florina admitted that more than one person had warned her about this man from the start. Alexandra said she had quickly rejected Florina's boyfriend when he attempted to gain her interest but had been afraid it would stir up trouble if she told Florina about the incident. Florina contested that she needed to be told the truth for her own good so that she could let go of a person who wasn't honest with her. They understood that while they both had valid points, they were wrong in letting external influences come between their otherwise loving, sisterly bond.

After their listening session, the sisters hugged and apologized. Alexandra promised to be open and honest with Florina if she were ever to find herself in a similar situation, and Florina quickly dumped her two-timing boyfriend. Most important, the problem did not recur because both Alexandra and Florina had learned what they did wrong and worked to avoid it in future situations.

Now, my husband and I had no need to deport any of our girls to another country, and we could go back to sustaining our loving jungle of a family.

(I still had not a clue how my estranged cousin was related to me. . . .)

Just as in the argument between Alexandra and Florina, the larger-than-life bond of family shines through sorrows and joys alike. The connection of parent and child, especially, is a light that cannot be dimmed, no matter the distance between the two. Parent/child relationships are complex, intense, and powerful, at best. They require not only patience, but an understanding of both their psychological and karmic elements.

For example, if we take into account the karma of parent/child relationships, we begin to understand that people can reincarnate into a different gender and that parents and children may reverse roles in their next life together. Yes, you heard right. This turns the tables as parents become children again and vice versa. It all depends on the karma shared among the family members and the way in which it plays out in time. A child may choose to reincarnate as his or her parents' own parent in the next life so as to take care of them and return the love that they received. Or a parent and child may reincarnate as siblings in their next lives so as to experience a different dynamic on a more equal level. A mother who is not able to love her child, because of whatever psychological component, may need to reincarnate as the child to a parent so as to experience that kind of love before she can extend it to another. Familial positions shift throughout our lives based on karmic need. Whatever dynamic is needed to repair or heal karma will be manifested through changing roles in our cycle of lives on earth.

Many parents who aren't biological parents to their children feel the same—a mother who adopts a child, or a father who enters a child's life through marriage, may feel as if being that child's parent was destiny. That's because the stepparent or adoptive parent was in fact the child's biological parent in a former life. The connection is no less powerful just because time has elapsed or the souls have reincarnated into new bodies. On the contrary, the need of the two souls to be together only intensifies.

I, for example, knew I had a karmic relationship with my stepdaughters. As I said before, they were meant to be my daughters in this life just as much as Alexandra was. I knew this from the moment my late husband told me their birthdays, and I quickly summed up their divine codes. (He would always stare at me strangely when I did this, not understanding my talk of karma, codes, spirit communication, and the like.) Carmen, the younger of the two, was born on 11/08/1976, which makes her life path a number 6 if you add up the digits. She was born the same month and day as Alexandra, who is my and Virgil's biological daughter. Carmen has a 2 in the month of her birth, and I have a 2 in my year of birth (1955 added up equals a 2). This showed me somewhat of a personal connection with Carmen, but I recognized a stronger one with Florina, and, in fact, Florina was always more open with me. Florina was born on 11/04/1975, which means her ruling number is a 1. She also has a 2 in her month of birth, but more interesting, my mother, my late husband, my sister, and Florina were all number 1s! And they all displayed the same traits: stubborn, independent, hardheaded, devoted, and loyal. I guess number 1s just follow me around, and I would have it no other way.

I also looked into the relationship both girls shared with their father, Virgil. They experienced two totally different relationships with him: Carmen's code is a 6 and Virgil was born in 1950, which is also a 6, clearly denoting that they knew each other in a past life. Florina is a 1 as Virgil was, which meant they resembled each other very closely in both physical looks and in their behavioral tendencies. But interestingly, Virgil shared a much stronger bond with his daughter Carmen, which became increasingly evident over time. Virgil's relationship with each of his daughters was made evident through numerology. This serves as another reminder of the synchronicities of our world, and how we can discover them ourselves by using numbers and karma.

What are the joys of your family? What synchronicities do you see among its members? Do you see the lessons that each person, especially your children or parents, came to teach you?

Allowing Your Children Freedom

One word is inseparable from parenthood, and that is *sacrifice*—parents naturally want to give to and care for their children without limits. Simply put, we want to give them the world. But how much sacrifice is too much? When are you being too generous or too permissive for their own good? When does sacrificing your desires for theirs cross the limits of good parenting and become self-destructive for both parents and children?

Of course, children can also sacrifice tremendously to be a "dutiful" son or daughter, too. How do you balance each other's need for freedom and need to do things "my way" with what you want the other to do?

When it comes to granting your parent or child freedom, you have to weigh the karmic implications of your choices. It's important to sacrifice within healthy bounds. If you're a parent, do not attempt to interfere with the personal karma of your children. If you do sacrifice too much, you merge your karma with that of your children and you create more bad karma for them than good. That's because you can block them from learning the lessons they have to learn, and from going through the experiences, however difficult, that they were meant to pass through in this life. Your journey is your own, and while you can help clear the path for your loved ones, you can't carry them on your shoulders down the road.

When I, Carmen, heard that my daughter Alexandra wanted to get a tattoo, I was beside myself. I instantly knew it was a big mistake Alexandra would come to regret. But I didn't interfere with Alexandra's decision—although I tried to talk (beg) her out of it, Alexandra insisted a tattoo would make her happy. So I did what no other parent in her right mind would have done: I went with her to the tattoo parlor and held her hand through the procedure. The entire time we were there, I could hear my late mother's spirit hissing in my ear, "Are you crazy?! What are you letting this child do?!" My own mother (who, as I explained before, was overly protective and sacrificing because she didn't grow up with a mother figure in her life) literally would have killed me if I'd told her I wanted to permanently ink a mythical creature onto my breast. But I knew better than to lock Alexandra in her room and throw away the key so she couldn't get the tattoo. This was one of Alexandra's karmic lessons to learn in this life—the lesson of worshipping her body instead of tarnishing it. She would come to get several more tattoos throughout her youth—as well as piercings, which she later let close up.

When the tattoo was completed, Alexandra stood proudly in front of the mirror, admiring her new bodily work of art, content that she had accomplished her rebellious task. I shook my head with a half smile and said simply, "If this is what you want, my dear." She answered, "Of course it's what I want. I'm the coolest girl in school now!" Like a wise mother I replied, "There will come the day when you will have it removed." Alexandra rolled her eyes as we walked out of the tattoo parlor. Needless to say, I didn't tip the artist.

Ten years later, Alexandra was desperately running to laser session after laser session to have her tattoo removed. (Mother is always right, isn't she?) The procedures didn't go so well, unfortunately, and Alexandra was left with a scar in place of the tattoo. But she understands that she had a personal karmic lesson to learn about caring for her body as for a temple. While she does regret getting the tattoo, she thanks me for allowing her to learn her lesson without interference. Had I forbidden her to get the tattoo, she says, she would have acted out in other, possibly more harmful ways. Or maybe she would have gone to an illegal parlor that was willing to tattoo a minor, which would have been far more dangerous. She also would have harbored resentment toward me for my refusal. So as much as this tattoo permanently scarred Alexandra, both physically and emotionally, it served as a karmic obstacle she needed to overcome. Alexandra does insist, however, that if her own future children ever bring up the idea of getting a tattoo, she will lock them in their room and throw away the key without a second thought.

On the other end of the spectrum, again, children can sacrifice too much for their parents, too, relinquishing their freedom in order to be dutiful and please Mom and Dad. They can give up on their personal dreams because they may interfere with what their parents want them to do in life. I remember a client named Steve who came to me some time ago. Steve sat down in my office, sweating in frustration, and began to explain that he was sixty-one and had never been married. Steve told me his father had died when he was young and since then, Steve took complete care of his mother, who never remarried. Even in his adulthood, Steve's mom did everything for him—from his laundry to cooking dinner to cleaning his apartment. Steve needed to spend time with his mother every afternoon after work, which hindered his chances of having a strong social life and meeting a woman. Steve never meant any harm, as he only wanted to help and protect his mother—to be the "dutiful" son who does the right thing—but he was impeding his own personal life without even realizing it. Steve said he didn't mind his mother's constant presence and aid but added that he didn't understand why he had never been able to attract a stable, lasting relationship into his life when he so dearly wanted one.

I asked Steve if he thought the karmic complications with his mother had anything to do with him not being able to build a family of his own. He said he'd never thought of it that way. However, it was clear to me that Steve's mother's karmic interference prevented him from being able to have his own true love. Steve's mother, unfortunately, passed about a year after he began coming to see me. And interestingly, Steve finally got married shortly afterward. Steve was only able to build a romantic life for himself without the karmic involvement of his mother. Once the karma with his mother was cleared, he became energetically free to pursue a love relationship for himself.

Had Steve recognized that he and his mother shared karma that needed to be cleared in order for him to move forward in his personal life, I believe he would have been able to enjoy a happy marriage much sooner. Even so, he had learned from his mother a pattern of overdependence on the one you love, and that karmic lesson had to be mastered in his relationship with his new wife.

Setting and Maintaining Healthy Boundaries

You can do several things to achieve a healthy degree of separation from others—whether they're your parents or your children, or even your partner or a close friend—so that they can't negatively influence your well-being. Evaluate which of these actions you must take in any given situation to limit the emotional impact of others upon you.

MEDITATE AND REFLECT TO MODULATE
YOUR EMOTIONS

Many times it is we who stir the pot of drama. Our own escalating emotions can quickly turn a day out into a disaster, which is why, when you leave the house, don't just check if you have your cell phone and wallet—check how you feel and why you feel this way. Take a moment and ask yourself: Do I feel tense, irritable, or stressed today? Will these feelings create friction with others or make it difficult for me to enjoy myself? If the answer is yes, take a deep breath and clear your heart and mind of any lingering anger, irritation, or frustration before stepping out to be in the company of others. A quick five-minute meditation will help relax you and turn your mood from anxious to excited. (And if you live with a parent or child, do this emotional check-in throughout the day to keep the emotional waters in your home calm.)

SETTLE OLD DIFFERENCES

If there's been discord between you and someone else, don't leave the situation unsettled—particularly if the conflict is between you and your parent or child. Old problems tend to become recurring problems. Make a list of anyone with whom you share unresolved conflict—friends you don't see eye to eye with, family members who make you irate, even people with whom you've had a bad falling-out. Remember, all your relationships affect one another. A spat with your mother will affect your relationship with your daughter, even if they live many miles apart. Promise to resolve these differences you have with others one way or another, even if it's sending the individuals on your list a quick e-mail wishing them well and sending them peace. Detach from negative memories by surrendering your ego and stating to the other person that you hold no grudges. You will feel a surge of serenity when you truly forgive and forge ahead.

REFRAIN FROM PROVOCATION

There is no need to give in when someone is pushing your buttons. Take a deep breath and commit to resolving the situation within yourself before asking the other person to change his or her behavior. Disengage your buttons! Work on your own issues and then say, gently, "I know you probably don't realize it, but when you do [name the behavior], I feel [name how you feel]." Give the other person the benefit of the doubt and an opportunity to apologize and shift his or her behavior. Don't take the behavior personally and insist, "You're disrespecting me! You have no respect for me." Your child or mother may be disrespecting you in that moment but have deep respect for you overall. Again, don't automatically take the behavior personally. Whenever someone provokes you, be the bigger person and don't engage in a heated conflict. Get to the bottom of what's really going on.

Distract yourself from your emotions when you feel an argument coming on by reminding yourself that you are above getting ugly with someone else. If it's your parent or child who has hurt your feelings, remember that squabbles up and down the family tree are inevitable. You chose to be closely related in this life so that you could learn from each other. Walking away from an argument instead of giving in to it will command respect and recognition and open the doors for love and kindness to flow freely again.

SET LIMITS FOR YOURSELF

Setting boundaries includes not attending a gathering where you know you'll encounter someone who clashes with you every time you're in the same room. On some level, you will want to go to the family gathering, of course—we know how precious family is meant to be. But all those relatives, and the potential for emotional conflict—the reunion of individuals with egos can be daunting!

Setting boundaries means protecting yourself from egos that have been triggered by old issues and karma that is probably carried over from past lifetimes. It means making choices like not drinking to the point of doing something you'll later regret, and not letting your frustration build without taking some time out to defuse your anger. Whenever possible, avoid situations that are bound to become bad ones. Know the limits of your patience. If your family is driving you crazy lately, and you are under a lot of stress, limit your interactions until the emotions have settled a bit and as a group, and you are better able to tolerate each other's peccadillos. Limit the amount of time the gathering lasts, and make it easy for family members to take their leave without a drama ensuing. Avoid the conversations and activities that always seem to lead to conflict. Relationships require a degree of discipline, and it becomes your responsibility to steer clear of scenarios that play on your weaknesses or push others' buttons. If Mom needs to cook the meal a certain way, stay out of the kitchen or be prepared to follow her orders as if you were in the army. If your daughter needs to handle her toddler's tantrum her way, step back. Do not rush in and trample a parent's or child's boundaries.

Conflict and Envy

Envy is the green-eyed monster that makes us miserable when others are happy, and happy when others are miserable. Envy is a completely ego-generated emotion that stems from our own insecurities. In my counseling practice, I, Carmen, see many female clients who struggle with not getting along with their child or children, in particular their daughters. And although it seems wrong in theory, because mothers should be unconditionally supportive and loving of their children, it's more common than you can imagine.

A few years ago, a client named Camilla walked into my office, seething with rage toward her daughter. When I asked her what her daughter had done to make her this angry, Camilla responded that her daughter had the audacity to become a fashion designer and get married. I blinked a few times, trying not to look shocked—clients are not usually that forthright about their resentments!—before asking Camilla what was so wrong about her daughter having a career and a family. Camilla replied that since she had never held a job and had gone through a divorce, her daughter shouldn't be able to enjoy such joys. She insisted that her daughter's marriage would surely end in divorce—"since most of them do," she said knowingly. She also insisted that her daughter's job was a waste of time because the girl hadn't gone to college to become a fashion designer, so she was "clearly wasting her fine education." Fed by hubris, Camilla was so envious of her daughter's success that she would have rather seen her daughter alone and broke than have her surpass Camilla in any way. Here, Camilla may seem like an awful person and parent, but we're all guilty of envious inklings to some degree.

Many parents haven't worked through their own issues about feeling victimized by life, so while they love their children and want the best for them, they can't quite get comfortable with their sons' and daughters' success. To heal the relationship and the bad karma created by envy, a parent has to eliminate her own insecurities so that she doesn't feel resentment toward the child she raised for possibly doing "better" than her.

The mother-daughter bond is the most intense and powerful bond there is. And as anyone who's experienced an intense bond can tell you, it's not all positive. The especially deep nature of a mother-daughter bond leads to some naturally occurring conflict, jealousy, and ambivalence. That's because among women a certain degree of competition, whether conscious or subconscious, is always embedded in our DNA.

Mother-daughter relationships are often disturbed by issues of identity. Women often say, "I don't want to end up like my mother," yet they don't realize that they are, of course, going to be like their mothers. (Who else would they be like, their first-grade teacher?) Blood is blood, after all. They possess the free will to change the course of their lives, but nothing is guaranteed. Maybe a woman hates the fact that her mother's marriage failed and resulted in a divorce, so she will do everything to avoid that.

Yes, it's totally doable to change the family karma. But she will have to work extra hard to prevent her own divorce. And with time, she may learn that there are circumstances in life that are beyond her control. There is a struggle to keep yourself both apart from and within the mother figure in your life.

This can happen even among fathers and their sons; a father may subconsciously struggle with the fact that his son is doing better than him, perhaps because he's taken over the family business and has made it grow more than the father ever could. The notion of a child "surpassing" his or her parent can cause the parent to feel notions of resentment, which may be deeply submerged. Of course, all parents want what's best for their children, and wish them success and luck, but it's within human nature to feel a twinge of envy, even toward one's children, and this stems from our pride. But what are the healthy limits of parent-child rivalries?

The best way to eliminate any sort of jealousy or animosity toward your child is to understand first that this feeling is normal to a certain degree and then evaluate its source. This requires a bit of honest introspection and reflection into your own past as a child. Ask yourself: Were my parents always happy for me? Can I remember a time when either one seemed at all jealous or resentful toward my success? What did I feel when this happened? Do I harbor any such feelings toward my children? Probing into your own jealous tendencies, however scarce they may be, allows you to identify and eliminate their source.

ALEXANDRA

The Family Blender

I was part of a blended family. There were animals (lots of them), stepchildren and stepparents, relatives-in-law, Christians, Jews, Romanians, Israelis, Puerto Ricans, children and grandparents, and a strangely disappearing "family cousin" named Silviu. (No one understood how he was related to the family, but we took him in anyway. He usually slept on the couch.) And I can tell you that it got a little crazy sometimes. But we recognized one thing— we were family, and that was quite enough to allow us to see past our different backgrounds or beliefs and make us happy.

My father loved to throw big family dinners on Mondays. There were my half sisters and their children, chatting away about mutual friends and chiding their children for eating with their hands. Beside them sat their tall, dark, and handsome Latino husbands, clucking to each other rapidly in their native tongue. My father was perched at the head of the table like a king on a throne, his thick black hair and thick lips characteristic among his three Romanian brothers, all of whom were present and all of whom had married women from Israel. (In some families, that would be seen as coincidental. In mine, of course, my mother told a story about our karmic connection with Israel.) My mother delegated the passing down of dishes and heaped more food onto everyone's plate whether they liked it or not. My lesbian aunt and her partner were found on the opposite end, faithfully holding hands and partaking in the familial tomfoolery. Beneath the table lurked several cats and dogs, waiting to surface their snouts at the first opportunity of a hand holding scraps of meat. And of course there was Silviu, the mysterious family cousin, giggling at everyone's jokes, though some were in Spanish or Hebrew, which he did not speak.

To a passerby who peered through the window, we might have looked like a conglomeration of people just sitting at a table. But in our home there was a cluster of kind smiles, laughter bursting forth at inside jokes, hearty pats on the back, and fond memories recounted together. We were a strange blending of different beings all longing for the same thing—to love and to be loved. We shared not just food and a communal table—we shared love lit by the light of our souls. Such were my family dinners, my Monday evenings, my most sorely missed memory.

I hear many people complain about their family members: "My sister's a . . . ," "My aunt did this," "I can't stand my dad." And although I expressed similar frustrations growing up, I shake my head at their words, envious that they have these family members in their lives and take their presence for granted. How I wish to be as close to my half sisters as in our youth, see my aunt who now lives in Europe, or hug my dad once more! I even miss Silviu, who finally found a different home (though we do not know where).

I've learned that family feuds are perfectly normal, but what is not normal are the permanent rifts we allow to come between us. Arguments and differing opinions shouldn't lead to painful separations. Sooner or later, life makes us all regret our pride and stubborn nature.

Nearly five years have passed since my father left this world and left our family dinners. We have tried to come together as before, but the food, however flavorful, was tasteless without his presence. In my father's honor, I share my six keys to maintaining familial peace and giving to and receiving the most of your family.

ALEXANDRA'S SIX KEYS TO ENJOYING YOUR FAMILY
PUT YOUR PRIDE ASIDE

Pride is the number one cause of familial grief. That's because our ego, the generator of our pride, makes us stubbornly hold on to the notion that we and only we can be right. Pride comes between families in ugly ways. It can simply devastate a family because the members begin to see themselves as individuals disassociated from the whole. Pride causes us to lose the sense of unity and only look out for ourselves. Many of my mom's clients say they haven't spoken to their parent or sibling in years. When she asks them why, she usually receives a "proud" answer: "They hurt me . . ." or "They did this to me. . . ." The answer always implies a "me" factor—that is pride showing its ugly head. Pride makes us do foolish things we regret—like getting huge tattoos! But it should never cause us to ostracize someone we care about.

In a family, it's easy to find reasons not to get along—after all, just because we're family doesn't mean we're not completely different people. There were many different "voices" in ours when I was growing up. But by letting go of pride and having a sense of humor about our conflicting ideas and preferences, we were able to remain close. Don't be so proud that you allow a resolvable matter to become a karmic rift in your family.

Give People Time

Change requires time. People may need to change, but it takes a while for them to see this and begin to work on themselves. Change is a process, not a result. The best thing you can do for a family member who is difficult to handle is to gently push them toward the changes they need to make. But be patient! Take your time with them and offer your unconditional support.

The best way to help someone change is by showing them what change looks like—change yourself to reflect the behaviors they need to work on. If you have a family member who is always bad-mouthing everybody, don't indulge in this behavior yourself. Tell them you won't partake in gossip or spreading negative words about others. In time, they'll understand they can't get away with it in front of you. They may even come to understand that what they're doing is wrong and modify their behavior. In the meantime, don't nag them or criticize them constantly. Allow them to evolve at their own pace.

The same goes for any other behavior that you don't like. Parents can model behavior to children, but children can certainly model behavior to parents as well. If your parents are "set in their ways," love them and respect them, but gently demonstrate to them there is another way. Parents can get very defensive if their children point out their failings. Be kind and loving even if their behavior bothers you a lot. Simply go about doing it your way. They are paying attention even if their pride causes them to pretend that they aren't.

Rising above the behaviors of others sets you up as an example for change. Just remember that this doesn't happen overnight, and that your patience may be tested as the people in your family perform their own inner work. But this gives you a chance to expand your own threshold of patience and tolerance for others, which in turn makes you a better, more evolved person. What's important is that you will see progress in time.

Wear Their Shoes

As they say, "Be kind, for everyone you meet is fighting a battle you know nothing about." You have to try to imagine what it's like to wear someone else's shoes and walk their path in life. And even if you think you can imagine it, it's probably still nothing like you imagine. It's easy to pinpoint the shortcomings of your family members—they may be judgmental, hypocritical, or annoying. But it's more difficult to understand the roots of their weaknesses. You might think you know them well because you lived with them for years, but you can't truly know what is going on in another person's heart. You haven't lived that person's life.

Perhaps your parent is judgmental of your relationship because she sees you going through an experience that's similar to a negative one she went through in her youth. Your family wants what's best for you, but they may have trouble expressing that or may go about it in a completely inappropriate way. When you understand this, you learn not to take too personally their words and actions that may be out of line. You begin to see the roots of their weaknesses surface. And to see the bare wound of someone's failings is to see the most intimate part of their being. Appreciate that.

Many years ago, when my mom was still in training as a counselor, she used to work alongside a prominent therapist and counselor. The two sometimes did sessions together, and one day, a beautiful young woman walked in for a session. She began to talk about how she was in love with a married man who seemed to be in love with her too, but that this sort of relationship caused her much grief. Now, normally Carmen would have advised this young woman to seek a love that was free and that she could call her own. She would not have commented on the morality of her choice, as that wasn't her place. As someone who hears the most intimate details of her clients' lives, my mom has vowed never to judge anyone, even silently, no matter how morally "wrong" their decisions might seem. She's always reminded herself that everyone is fighting personal battles each day, and she is neither different nor better. We can never hope to comprehend fully someone else's situation unless we've walked a mile in their shoes, especially when it comes to the complexities of love. So all my mom can do is offer her guidance toward the best resolution to any given problem, which is why so many people turn to her for help.

Given the tears streaming down this young client's face and her honest declarations of love for the married man, Carmen would have guided her toward this advice very gently and compassionately, so as not to hurt her even more. She would have empowered her so that she could realize her self-worth rather than breaking her down to the harsh truth that she was in a dead-end situation, as this was bound to cause her more pain and probably make her retreat into denial. But before Carmen could open her mouth to offer her sagelike advice, the therapist she was training with rolled her eyes and blurted out, "Are you kidding me? Do you think for a second he really loves you? He's married—he couldn't care less about you! He'll never call you again!" The therapist went on and on with words that were hurtful even for Carmen to hear. By the time she was done, the client's minor tears had turned into sobs. This was only deepening her wound. Carmen was very upset with the other therapist but didn't feel she could say anything during the session. She would have to talk to her afterward.

When the session ended, as much as my mom wanted to reprimand her partner about the treatment of their client, she reminded herself to wear her partner's shoes. She thought about her experiences and then understood: this therapist had been married for many years to a man who carried out a public affair with a young woman (a young woman who, strangely enough, somewhat resembled the one who had been sitting in the chair in front of them). Subconsciously, the therapist was releasing her rage—pent up for many years from her own bad experience—on this poor girl.

In theory, being with a married man is wrong, yes. But the therapist was still in pain from the wounds of her own tragedy, and it reflected plainly in her chiding of her client. Her weaknesses surfaced, as weaknesses often do. Though the client left somewhat traumatized, Carmen understood where the therapist was coming from, so she was able to gently approach her about how she handled their clients and talk about how they could begin to fix the situation. She saw the roots of her weaknesses and didn't take her words or actions personally (though I'm pretty sure that poor client did). This story more than any other reminds me that we must try to wear each other's shoes, even if the size doesn't fit, to understand where others are coming from before resorting to judgment or blame. You will find that this holds especially true in terms of family members, whose actions might seem questionable because they are in the midst of their own battles.

Appreciate Generational and Cultural Differences

I sometimes have trouble understanding my generation, who hold the mistaken notion that if you hang out with your parents or grandparents, you aren't "cool" (or don't have "swag," or whatever the term may be). I openly admit that my mother is my best friend. She is the only reason I am as wise as I am. She's given me everything I have and has made me who I am. So why in the world would I have an issue with our generational gap? I would much rather spend my time with her than my friends, because she helps me evolve and expand my being. But to many young people, spending time with the older generations is seen as a chore and not a pleasure. There is so much we can learn about bettering our lives from those who have already gone through life. Why ignore their wisdom?

In fact, I often blurt out Romanian proverbs and sayings I picked up from my parents or grandparents: things like, "Don't mix up your jars of pickles" (meaning, don't mix up your affairs). Most of my friends will just look at me when I say such things and ask me where in the world I got that from.

Obviously, as mother and daughter, and as two people who grew up in two very different places and very different times, my mom and I have had opposite experiences. And frankly, I've found that people my age in America can have quite a different mentality from people of my age in Romania, and I'm not completely in sync with the mind-set of either group. In the United States, children are taught independence and to think for themselves. While these principles are positive and valuable to a certain degree, they can also keep people apart and feeling alienated. They can become standoffish, even closed, to receiving guidance, believing that depending on others or asking for help is somehow shameful. It's hard to develop a sense of community when independence is so revered. In most European and Latin cultures, however, community is everything. People learn and grow through each other—there is mutual support and effort. This, taken to the extreme, isn't positive either. But in general, it promotes bonding with people of different generations and backgrounds, which leads to stronger communities. And in terms of a family, appreciating the young and old alike and absorbing the unique wisdom of each family member will strengthen the bond of kinship.

BEWARE OF EXTERNAL INFLUENCES

External influences are often the cause of our family dramas. You may have problems with your mother because of your sister, or you argue with your mother-in-law or best friend because they are pressuring you to parent in a certain way. Whether we realize it or not, even friends and coworkers can play a big role in our family dynamic. As we said in Chapter 1, the energy of everyone around seeps into all of our relationships, often without our awareness. The best thing we can do is be mindful of our influences and separate our relationships as much as we can. This is not to say that you should distance yourself from your sister because she is sowing discord between you and your mother, or that you should cut off your mother-in-law or best friend because her advice is causing you stress. But when people's energy has become toxic, you can—and must—keep them at arm's length. Set firm boundaries. You may have to say, "I appreciate your concern and advice, and I'll consider it," and make a note to yourself not to discuss the situation with that person any further.

You can also compromise with the people affecting your relationships as well as those affected by them. Stand up firmly but politely against people who are negatively impacting your relationships. Show them love and compassion, but do not tolerate their unnecessary impressions on other aspects of your life. If your sister brings up your mother, simply tell her you won't have this discussion, that she should work it out with your mother, and change the subject. Then tell your mother you would rather not be pulled into her conflict with your sister.

At the end of the day, there's only so much you can do to control the actions of others. But you can rest assured that you've done everything possible to keep your karma clean and avoid creating negative karma, and that you have put in much considerable effort to repair your relationships through love and patience. If handled correctly, external influences don't need to create problems between you and other family members. And certainly keeping outside influences at bay will promote a more joyous familial dynamic.

Have Bonding Rituals

People sometimes wince at the idea of "family bonding," because they think it entails seeing distant, somewhat irritating family members on birthdays or holidays, or at family reunions, under less-than-pleasant circumstances (too much alcohol plus too much complication over planning an event equals family quarrels). But family bonding can happen at any time, whether it's gathering to watch a movie together or simply walking the family dog down the block. Even arguments have their place in a family that wishes to have strong bonds—at least you share emotions with your family members. And the process of making up, healing, and learning after an argument can leave you closer than before if the family members are willing to cooperate and compromise. Parents and children are supposed to clash with each other at times—it's a given. Conflict is an opportunity for both parties to grow and master their karma. It also is an opportunity for developing greater trust and intimacy, which tightens family bonds. The key is to make the conflict as loving as possible—to be patient with each other and truly listen to and respect each other.

Bonding can occur whenever you spend time with your family

members, being attentive to their needs and trying to incorporate activities they like to do. You might think, "Ugh, I have to spend time with my father today." If you aren't completely familiar with his story and dread the experience, consider this: there's something to learn from everyone, whether you get along with them all the time or not. Inch your way to a stronger bond. It won't happen instantly. Becoming closer will take time, effort, repeated exposure, and patience. One day as you say good-bye to your father and you head back to your house, you might find yourself thinking, "Wow, did we just bond?"

The less you look at working at forming bonds as a chore, the less it becomes one, and the more it turns into a pleasure. Change your mentality from "I need to get along with this person" to "I want to get along with this person." Put effort into getting along with your parents and children. Ask them about their feelings and their stories. Do you know what your father wanted to be when he grew up, or whether his passions were encouraged? Do you know your mother's greatest disappointment, or your stepdaughter's biggest fear? Better yet, can you relate to any of their anecdotes or do you share similar experiences? Look past the behaviors that bother you and lovingly open your heart to their stories. There is a greater reason they are in your life—to help you master your karma. There is always a greater reason beyond the complications and disagreements and distance. Value them even if your bond is frayed.

And if you can't tolerate them at all because their behavior is too intense, wish them healing. Pray for them, and pray for yourself, too. Try to protect them while protecting yourself. Your karma will remain unstained, even through the rough relationship. Perhaps then the bond will be healed in this lifetime. If not, we promise you, when they cross over to the other side, what they feel toward you will be love—and regret that they were not more loving when they were here. Love them today, as they are, and don't forget to love yourself.

6

TO LOVE, OR
NOT TO LOVE?

(That Is the Karmic Question)

*The love we draw in is a reflection not of what
we want, but of what we lack.*

—DR. CARMEN HARRA

Husbands and wives can often do mini comedy routines about each other's flaws. It's wonderful to have someone who will turn annoyance into amusement over your binge watching episodes of a television show, misplacing house keys, taking forever to primp and get out of the house, or any number of quirky habits you may have. Sometimes a couple's differences will frustrate them to the point that they argue and become furious with each other. I, Carmen, drove Virgil crazy at times. And he might not have known it, but he certainly drove me crazy, too. At one point we owned a restaurant together, and Virgil kept a cat in its basement as a pet. Now, Virgil was such a strong—at times even cold—character that it's hard to imagine him showing affection to an animal. But I remember when that cat went missing, and Virgil closed the restaurant for two full days, paying all the employees to scour the neighborhood calling the cat's name (as the restaurant bills were piling up, mind you). Virgil's love for his pets really rubbed off on me, though—when the family dog, Valentino, went missing, I spent days searching up and down a wooded area, calling his name until someone in the neighborhood called the police on me. Thankfully I found him, and Alexandra—who was the culprit behind the dog's accidental, temporary escape—will have to spend the rest of her life apologizing to me for my near-arrest (the police were not sympathetic that I had lost my dog, or that I was heard screaming "Valentinoooo!" for hours on end). The point is that we can not only learn to live with our loved ones' quirks, we can develop similar ones ourselves. (And it's a good thing in this case—Virgil found his cat and I found my dog and Alexandra will never lose an animal again!)

So when you are tempted to nitpick your partner's tiny imperfections, just remember that nobody's perfect, and those who love you will do their best to make up for their failings. If we could drill this into your head, we would: *People will not give you what you want—they will give you what they can.* This is perhaps the greatest lesson of all relationships. If you can accept and understand each person's unique capacity for love, and each person's way of expressing that love, you can be happy.

When we enter a relationship we expect to get what we give. We expect the same amount and quality of love as we put in. But we are highly mistaken in believing that all people share the same capacity for love, or that they express love in the same way. Some people can love unconditionally. That's an amazing quality to possess and makes everyone's life easier. Others, though, can love in a more limited way. They may love deeply but be unable to express it, or they may express it in a way that others don't recognize their "language of love," as Harville Hendrix calls it.

Our hunger for more love can make us wear out a romantic partner. So can our habits, if we live with the one we love! But love nourishes the soul, so we put up with each other's failings. And when it comes to love, we seem never to be satisfied. Alas, we waste precious time trying to change our partners, make them conform to our needs and give us more affection and devotion. The more we push, the more we push the other person away. The key to happiness is understanding and accepting that each of us has a different experience of love—and that the ultimate source of love is God. If you reconnect to God by going within, you'll rediscover your primary source of love, which cannot be satiated with love from another person. Then, nourished by all-encompassing, divine love, you'll find yourself less needy and greedy in human relationships—not to mention more accepting of your partner's flaws and quirks, too.

Finding the Right Partner

One of the reasons we can push a partner too far is that we've chosen the wrong person for us. We do this out of fear that we will be alone and never find "Mr. Right" or "Ms. Right." Relationships take work, so it's crucial that you find the right partner rather than settle for someone who seems "good enough" but who turns out not to give you anywhere near as much love, loyalty, and affection as you need and desire.

If ever there was a secret to finding the right partner, it is this: *you must recognize that you deserve a wonderful partner, but also that you must work on yourself.* You can't be blindly expectant and think, "I'm the best. I deserve the best person." Yes, you do deserve the best, but you aren't "the best." You, like everyone, are imperfect. Deny that, and you're more likely to long for unattainable perfection in another. It's a way of avoiding the challenge of reflecting on yourself and working on your own flaws.

You need to become the best version of yourself so you can attract a person who will love you and treat you well. Finding the right partner starts with recognizing and resolving your karma. If you've attracted the same type of partner again and again and are frustrated, it's because your karma is drawing you to people who will push you to resolve your karmic issues.

Let's say you've only attracted partners who have taken advantage of you. Take a step back from yourself and examine yourself and your behavior. Do you give off an energy that invites others to take advantage of you? Are you too nice, kind, or trusting? You may need to protect yourself more and become more strong-willed, in control, and fearless. Being kindhearted and vulnerable doesn't have to mean you're easily fooled. Don't fear being vulnerable—fear being dishonest with yourself. Know your limits and your triggers. If you're a soft touch, be mindful of that propensity so you have more control over it. Take a look at your destiny code—are there issues you are fated to work on? It's time to get started if you haven't already!

Ultimately, we are not physical beings but energy beings—

that is the core of what composes us. This is a metaphysical truth! Matter is actually light energy, and our energy bodies are our souls. We know from science that opposites attract while objects with like charges repel. Nothing could be more true in the real world! If you are tired of falling for a certain type of person, then change who you are—because you're the one creating the charge that draws that type of person to you.

If you're not in a committed, romantic relationship, the most important thing you can do to find a partner is work on your karma and get out and be among people. The more friendships you make and the more you get out into your community, the better your chances of meeting someone. Being able to make new friends and get along with a variety of people will help you find the right partner for you.

Then, when you meet someone, if you have done work on yourself and your karma, you are less likely to let your insecurities and fear of being alone get in your way. Having seen the progress you've made toward erasing your flaws and correcting what's out of balance within you, you'll have greater confidence and be able to notice when you are starting to let your ego get the better of you.

When looking for partners, both genders make mistakes. A common trap men fall into is trying to impress the other person by talking continually about themselves and their major accomplishments. Yes, you are selling yourself, and a potential partner does want to know about you. However, you don't want to become a one-man show and leave the other person feeling ignored, disconnected, and discounted. This is when you might notice the woman reaching into her purse for her phone to type that *Help me, this guy's a weirdo* text to her best friend. (I, Alexandra, have received this text more than once!) The most typical problem that women have in trying to attract a partner is neediness. Insecurity and neediness are huge, *huge* turnoffs unless your love interest has an unhealthy need to be controlling and take care of you as if you were incompetent. People are attracted to those who have lives of their own and goals and ambitions—but who also still make plenty of time for that special someone.

If you find yourself obsessing over someone or overanalyzing your partner's every move, stop it! If you expect the other person to act and feel exactly as you do, or respond to you as you would respond to them, stop yourself. Everyone is different. Ask questions and spend time with each other, observing your partner. See how he acts with his mother and sister. See how she acts with her friends and family. If you are enamored with a man who is rude to waitresses, seems to hero-worship his mentor, is constantly battling with his brother, and thinks his mother is a saint at all times, run. These extreme behaviors reflect unresolved karma with him that will surely come to the surface in his relationship with you. Listen to your instincts and don't think you're the one person who will always be on his good side.

Relationships are best left detached from our fears and sustained by self-security, so if you're feeling insecure, don't run away from that uncomfortable feeling. Explore your patterns and your partners. If you always find yourself doubting a partner just when you start getting comfortable in the relationship, or the initial passion wears off, look at yourself in the mirror. The problem in the relationship is you and your unresolved karma.

CARMEN

The Truth of Your Relationship

As a psychologist and counselor for more than twenty years, I have heard every relationship problem on this planet. I have witnessed entire boxes of tissues being used by clients whose eyes poured forth emotion, and I've heard the bellowing wails belonging to the brokenhearted. Truly there is nothing that can hurt us quite like love.

Why do we fall in love if it hurts so much? Because relationships are the classroom in which we learn karmic lessons, and the powerful emotions that exist between us and our partners keep us tied together. Love is designed to push us into facing our karma and resolving it. If we work on our karma on our own, then we will resolve it to such a degree that our relationships won't be as dramatic, complicated, and painful. However, we tend to forget the pain of love when we're longing for it, and we focus on finding that special partner rather than working on ourselves. We should be doing both simultaneously!

Being human means being highly susceptible to our feelings, but the unpredictable tides of emotion can interfere with logic, leading us to partners who are bad news—or who cause us to stay in bad relationships. We perceive through a sentimental veil that filters out all the flaws in the other person. Out of habit, we empathize with the one we love, the one with whom we've made a habit of sleeping each night, the person we fret about and shower with our attention.

Overwhelming emotions can make us neglect the reality that not all relationships are meant to last as long as they do, and some aren't meant to happen at all. Heartfelt attachment drives us to extend temporary relationships to permanent time frames. It causes us to pressure someone to become a soul mate when that's simply not going to happen.

How do you know if someone is truly the one for you, a soul mate you are meant to be with? How do you know if a relationship is worth fighting and suffering for? Once you understand the four types of love relationships and evaluate under which category your own relationship falls, the answer comes easily. Each of the four types of romantic relationships serves a unique and necessary purpose, helping us to improve and evolve. There are transitory, karmic, compromise, and soul mate relationships (you've learned a bit about the karmic ones already—they can be intense!). You might experience only one kind of relationship throughout your life or you might move through the full range of four. It all depends on the curious interaction between fate and free will. Let's take a closer look at each type of relationship, so you can establish the truth about your own.

Transitory relationships act as a bridge between two phases of evolution in a person's life, bringing about change or easing the burden of major life shifts. For example, a girl in high school may mature into a woman with the help of a transitory relationship with a romantic partner she cares about deeply, but she has learned her first lessons in love—that relationship is meant to end when she goes off to college. A transient relationship after a long marriage has ended may help the divorced person cope with the loss of the marriage and begin to heal. Transitory relationships are almost always temporary, but they serve a great purpose in gently pushing a person from one level of self-transformation to the next. What you have to be careful of, however, is not creating too much karma in a transitory relationship. This is where it gets tricky—most of us who are in a transient relationship don't know it. We see the relationship as one that's brimming with the full potential of any other type of relationship. So we invest in it—our time, emotions, efforts, and even money. There are three ways to recognize that your relationship is transitory:

1. You immediately enter a relationship after ending a long relationship, such as settling for the first person who shows interest after going through a breakup or divorce.
2. Your relationship is largely based on physical intimacy but lacks communication and soulful engagement.
3. There is a significant gap in age, financial standing, or mental attitude.

If you are in a transient relationship, understand its limits and be careful committing yourself fully to a bond that comes with a short expiration date.

Unlike transitory relationships, *karmic relationships* always entail some form of action that must play out between the partners. They are meant to break a pattern or cycle of recurring situations.

After the karma is resolved, however, the relationship may come to an end, as its purpose has been met. Such was the case in Alexandra's relationship with her most recent boyfriend. (She's not happy I'm bringing up this example.) After several years of dating the same person, Alexandra simply "woke up" one day and knew it was time to cut the ties. Their karmic mission had become complete. I myself had a karmic relationship with Virgil. I knew without a doubt that he was my soul mate from the moment I met him, but I also knew we had a specific karma to reenact and that we would be together for a very long time. (Alexandra is patiently awaiting her soul mate, and thinks that because of my intuitive abilities, I'll recognize her "Mr. Right" even before she does, which she finds somewhat annoying.) Karmic relationships are enriching experiences that can be progressive, elevating, and fulfilling, whether temporary or for the long term.

A *compromise relationship* is the most common of the four kinds of relationships, and it occurs when two people come together based on an arrangement of comfort, such as financial or emotional stability. Many relationships that are meant to end continue on because both partners have become very used to each other's habits and used to the stability of their relationship, so they find it difficult to part ways. In short, they settle for each other. They may have children, which makes them feel even more strongly that they're supposed to stay together, though neither may be fully happy or in love.

Relationships based on a compromise keep us stuck in a comfort zone that can become stultifying and very uncomfortable, yet we cling to the familiar. It's important to evaluate whether we're truly happy with our partner or merely remaining in the relationship out of habit. People often declare that their spouse is a great parent to their children but that they know deep down their relationship is a compromise.

Many people can feel in their hearts that they are in a compromise relationship but push the inkling aside. Some compromise relationships last a lifetime because neither partner wants to let go of the other or face the possibility of being alone or the scary unknown of life after this partner. Though the problem in compromise relationships is that one or both partners may not be completely satisfied, the decision to stay or to go is one's own.

A *soul mate (or soulful) relationship* reaches far deeper than the physical or emotional level. Soul mate relationships are few and far between, but when they do occur, they often pass the test of time. This kind of relationship is marked by an intense connection between two people, one that may even be difficult to convey in words. Two people just "get each other" and have a meeting of minds and souls. They may finish each other's sentences, even if they've known each other just a short time. They are best friends, two puzzle pieces that interlock perfectly. They feel a sense of "us against the world." Like anyone, soul mates will experience problems in their relationship, but they will be able to resolve their issues more easily than couples who aren't bound by soulful ties.

Soul mates may not have unresolved karma created in a previous lifetime. If they knew each other in their past lives, they may have created a lot of positive karma together. Perhaps they agree to meet up again, to generate more good karma and resolve any lingering bad karma.

I recognize that my relationship with Virgil was both karmic *and* soulful, for we were soul mates who had created karma together for many lifetimes. Although we had karma to resolve together, and we worked out quite a lot of it, we still felt a powerful connection to each other that did not diminish with time. Our love grew stronger and our emotional intimacy and trust deepened.

For some, a karmic relationship may be transitory (a brief romance until a past-life karma is resolved). It may be a compromise relationship, too (two people compromise to be together while they also share or have created karma). The only two relationships that can't be combined are compromise and soul mate— a soulful bond is never based on compromise for money, status, or personal advantage. Likewise, a compromise relationship can never hope to experience the unyielding love of a soulful relationship.

Relationships may also change over time. A transitory or compromise relationship may become karmic in nature as both partners have created karma together (establishing a family, sharing experiences and finances, and so on). Or a transitory relationship may turn into a compromise if both partners choose to stay together after their time in that relationship is up. Relationships are utterly predestined, yet they leave us so much room for free will. Isn't that amazing, how certain people are put right in front of us for specific reasons, yet we can choose and even change their roles in our lives? This unfathomable fusion of chance and choice is a large part of the beauty of life.

CARMEN

The Superpower of Soul Mates

How can you know whether your partner or potential partner is a soul mate? As the American writer Richard Bach said, "A soul mate is someone who has locks that fit our keys, and keys to fit our locks. When we feel safe enough to open the locks, our truest selves step out and we can be completely and honestly who we are."

Soul mates are the epitome of love and partnership. In our fast-paced, chaotic world, which boasts all sorts of different people, we find ourselves skimming through more relationships than we'd like in order to find that one person who can truly open our locks.

Not just anyone can fulfill you the way your soul mate can. A soul mate makes you feel entirely whole, healed, and intact—like no piece is missing from the puzzle. A life partner can be a great supporter and longtime companion but is limited in his or her ability to enrich your spirit. That captivating intimacy and karmic glue just aren't there.

Most of us remain in life-partner relationships because we "settle," for a multitude of reasons. First, we may have a real subconscious fear of being alone. And since we're biologically designed to fall in love, it's only natural that we pair up in this world. But we sometimes prolong what are meant to be temporary relationships and mistakenly settle into them for good. Some relationships must last for a certain period of time to close out a karmic chapter of life, relationships in which we're meant to have children with our partner but not necessarily remain with them, and some relationships are just plain confusing because a melting pot of emotions doesn't allow us to see our predestined path.

Throughout my career, I have seen everything from couples who married their childhood loves to people in their retirement years who still struggle with commitment issues. Most of us fall somewhere between these two extremes, meaning that we experience several relationships before finding the person we believe to be our perfect pairing. Whether you're currently married, in a relationship, or contemplating entering a relationship with a new love interest, it is crucial that you know what role this person will play in your life. After all, there's no avoiding the inevitable, often uncomfortable question we must ask ourselves: Is this the person I was bound by destiny to share my life with—or did I settle too quickly into a relationship with someone who can never complete me? Answering this question honestly can be hard without a bit of guidance. There are ten signs that indicate a soul mate bond (or a lack of) between you and your partner.

Ten Ways to Know If They're Your Soul Mate

1. *You just . . . know.* Describing how a soul mate makes you feel is difficult. It's a tenacious, profound, and blissfully lingering emotion that no words can encompass.

2. *Flashbacks.* If your partner is your soul mate, chances are he or she has been present in at least one of your past lives. Soul mates often choose to come back to-

gether during the same lifetime and scope each other out in the big world. You might suddenly and briefly experience flashbacks of your soul mate. You might even feel an odd sense of déjà vu, as if the moment in time has already taken place, perhaps a long time ago, perhaps in a different setting.

3. *You just "get" each other.* Ever met two partners who finish each other's sentences? Some people call that spending too much time together, but it's the signal of a soul mate connection. You might experience this with your best friend or your mother, but it is the telltale sign of a soul mate when you experience it with your romantic partner.

4. *You fall in love with his or her flaws.* No relationship is perfect, and even soul mate relationships will experience ups and downs. Still, that bond will be much harder to break. Soul mates have an easier time of tolerating—even learning to love—each other's imperfections. Your relationship is more likely to be a soul mate match if you both love each other exactly as you each are, accepting both the great and awful tendencies we all have.

5. *It's intense.* A soul mate relationship may be more intense than normal relationships, in both good and sometimes bad ways. The most important thing is that even during negative episodes, you're focused on resolving the problem and can see beyond the difficult moment.

6. *It feels like "you and me against the world."* Soul mates

often see their relationship as "us against the world." This doesn't mean they isolate themselves from others, but that they feel so linked together that they're ready and willing to take on any facet of life, so long as they are at each other's side.

7. *You are mentally inseparable.* Soul mates often have a mental connection similar to the kind that twins have with each other. One might pick up the phone to call the other at the exact same time. They often can intuit when something is wrong with the other, even when they are miles apart. Though you may be at a distance, your minds will always be in tune if you are soul mates.

8. *You feel secure and protected.* Regardless of the gender of your partner, he or she should always make you feel secure and protected. This means that if you're a heterosexual man, yes, your woman should make you feel protected, too! Your soul mate will make you feel like you have a guardian angel by your side. A person who plays on your insecurities, whether consciously or subconsciously, is most certainly not your soul mate.

9. *You can't imagine your life without him (or her).* A soul mate is not someone you can walk away from that easily. It is someone you can't imagine being without, a person you firmly believe is worth sticking with and fighting for.

10. *You look each other in the eye.* Soul mates have a tendency to look into each other's eyes when speaking more often than ordinary couples do—they almost "read" each other this way. It comes naturally from the

deep-seated connection between them. Looking a person in the eye when speaking denotes a high level of comfort and confidence in them.

Whether you and your partner are destined to be soul mates is decided by the universe—and perhaps two people who feel drawn to each other can, over the course of lifetimes, create that destiny for themselves. If you and your partner are simply two loving people who have settled for each other's strengths and weaknesses, there's nothing wrong with that. The beauty of free will is that you can remain in or change any relationship as you see fit. However, to be with your soul mate is one of the precious rarities of life, so don't settle too quickly when your soul mate may still be out there. Stay present in your relationship and make note of any problems to be corrected. Too often, out of fear of loneliness, people will remain in a relationship that is not nourishing and miss out on the opportunity to find a better one or even to find their soul mate.

Romantic relationships play critical roles in our lives. When it comes to deciding whether to stay in a relationship that isn't all that you hope it can be, perhaps the most difficult task lies in being honest with yourself about the core function of the relationship. Are the two of you together to be soul mates or to resolve karma—whether it's individual karma or shared karma? Is this relationship too unsatisfying of a classroom for learning your karmic lesson?

As you ponder your relationship, consider how the karma you and your partner have fits into group karma shared or created with others. It's possible that you would be much happier and more fulfilled in the relationship if you were able to get rid of outside influences that are affecting it.

Three's a Crowd—Four or More Is a Swarm

Couples don't exist in a vacuum. At any given moment, they are being influenced by many different energies. In fact, research shows that having other couples as friends can strengthen your romantic relationship. When each partner has same-sex friends they socialize with, it can take some of the pressure off their central romantic relationship. No one person can be everything to you, even if that person is your soul mate. You must take a bit of time off, too.

That said, it's important to be cautious about how much you share with others about your marriage or romance to avoid having other people become too involved in your partnership. Women especially can become overly dependent on asking their girlfriends for advice about their man troubles, and not be aware that their girlfriends have their own unresolved karma and can be very biased in their opinions. Do not—we repeat—**do not** believe everything your girlfriends tell you! Ask God for help, not Elizabeth or Jacqueline or Rachel.

You may have someone interfering in your relationship because there's group or shared karma to be worked out among all of you. Many times we don't even realize the extent to which someone else's involvement is affecting our relationship, until we get a rather rude wake-up call. I, Alexandra, have a loving, caring friend named Maritza. Maritza is so loving and caring that she deals as patiently and carefully with her husband as any woman can. But Maritza's husband is still, let's just say, "in the process of maturing" and has a lot to learn about relationships. Truth is, he makes it seem as if he cares more about being a part of his circle of friends than about his life at home. He did, however, buy Maritza a new car recently and insured it under his name. But Maritza's husband cares so much about one of his friends in particular that he also helped him buy a car and insured this vehicle under his name, too. I told him he should just become an auto financer, which he didn't find very funny. Regardless, the friend for whom he bought a car was so careless that he was mounting up weekly parking tickets and neglecting to pay them. This all came back on Maritza's husband's record. Maritza often joked that her husband and this friend care about each other so much, they must've been married in a past life (karmically speaking, it's possible).

One day, Maritza woke up and got ready for work as usual. She walked to her new car in a great mood, coffee in hand, to find that it had been booted. It turns out that her husband's friend had failed to pay more than fifteen parking tickets on his own car, insured under Maritza's husband's name. Now she was forced to pay over a thousand dollars to have the boot removed as well as cover her husband's friend's long-overdue tickets. Maritza knows she'll never recover that money, and her husband knows he might never recover her trust. This is a prime example of outside interference in a private relationship.

But what was Maritza to do to stop her husband's friend from interfering in their relationship? In this case, as her husband was unreceptive to her requests to please stop allowing his friend to come between them, there wasn't much she could do. She made the right decision—Maritza took a temporary break from her husband and left him all to his friend. Then, a week later, her husband lent his friend thousands of dollars in good faith so he could pay off the tickets he had accrued. His friend disappeared with the money, and once he realized that he'd been fooled, Maritza's husband began calling her asking for forgiveness.

Maritza's husband created bad karma with her by allowing a friend to come between them. He created good karma in trying to rectify the situation by lending his friend money to pay off the tickets, but his bad karma caused him to lose the money he lent. Sometimes, other people create karma with us and we can't do much to stop them. The best thing we can do in such instances is to try our very best to resolve the karma but then walk away temporarily. It then becomes up to the other person to realize their wrongdoings or continue to be blind to them.

Of course, it's not just friends who can interfere in relationships. Parents, siblings, adult children, and others (including car insurance companies) can, too—and so can people whose intent is not emotional intimacy but sexual satisfaction.

The Other Woman, the Other Man

Infidelity is the definitive relationship woe caused by outside influence. It's a source of drama and trauma for the person being cheated on and can also become hurtful to others because we're all interconnected. Surely, cheaters don't consider how their actions will affect their children or their partner's children, or how it might destroy friendships. Infidelity is a lesson we will all have to deal with sooner or later in life because even if cheating doesn't actually occur, temptation will.

Many women are terrified of the possibility of infidelity and believe it's the worst thing that can ever happen to them. There are far worse things that your partner can do to you than cheat. Typically, men and women see infidelity differently. To a man, cheating sexually may not involve any emotional intimacy—or so little that he is able to break off the relationship quickly when his partner finds out. A woman who cheats may be doing it passive-aggressively to prove something to herself or her partner, take revenge on her partner, or avenge her pain if she's been cheated on. This isn't always true—and of course, people who are attracted to a same-sex partner may follow the patterns of women or men. However, it's important to be aware of the fact that your partner may truly not see cheating in the way you see it. The affair may have meant little to your partner even if it is devastating for you to know that it occurred. It is difficult to do, but you must take infidelity as *impersonally* as possible.

It's also important to know that there's a karmic component behind most cases of infidelity. A person may cheat because he or she has in a prior life, or because he or she was partnered with that person in a past life. You may be cheated on more than once because you were a womanizer or heartbreaker in a previous life and you came into this life hoping to resolve the bad karma you created in that lifetime when you hurt other people.

Infidelity usually reflects some larger issue that is playing out. In terms of karma, it could be that you're in a transitional relationship that has become a compromise one that needs to end. Perhaps you and your partner fell out of love, or have a serious disagreement you have to work through. It's imperative to address the larger underlying issue and understand the causes of your partner's infidelity, rather than to become obsessed about it and cling to bitterness. Remember, though, some people are simply unfaithful because it's in their character or because they have bad karma to work through.

The great news is that many couples who have opted to work out their infidelity issues with their partner have, through mutual effort, become even stronger than before. To bring up a famous example, I, Carmen, knew Hillary wouldn't leave her husband, Bill Clinton, after his cheating scandal. First, according to their joint numerology, they weren't meant to split. Second, neither wanted to separate from the other. They do genuinely love each other, though he has a well-known weakness for women—a weakness rooted in his childhood experiences, where bad karma was created by his stepfather mistreating his mother. Bill and Hillary worked through their issues and, more than a decade after the infidelity scandal that caught the attention of an entire nation, they are still firmly together.

Hillary took much criticism for her decision, but none of us can know what it's like to be inside someone else's relationship. That's yet another reason to be cautious about letting someone else tell you how to manage your marriage or relationship. It's helpful to get insights from others, but you must ultimately make your own decisions. And in the case of infidelity, the choice is yours alone.

Karmic Sexuality, Sexual Attraction, and Gender Identity

When you have sex with someone, you create a karmic connection, whether you have emotional ties to that person or not. Why would you want to become energetically connected to people you don't know well and haven't built trust with? I, Alexandra, know several young women with HPV who weren't even promiscuous, but one wrong partner caused them the added karma of a lifelong disease. We are not supposed to have sex with many partners—and that's true of men and women.

Monogamous and long-term relationships are what we really yearn for, although we may not realize it. They fulfill us for much more than one night. Not everyone has to get married, but the extreme of too many partners is simply not good. It prevents you from creating deep emotional intimacy that comes from fidelity to your partner. Women and men who feel they need to have several partners to be satisfied are trying to prove something to themselves. And this is true regardless of whether you're heterosexual, homosexual, bisexual, or transgender—it's just a human truth. The instability of promiscuity stems from an inner instability.

Similarly, karma is reflected in all relationships. Being gay or lesbian often is the result of karma that a soul chooses to work out in this lifetime. I, Carmen, watched my sister, Mona, struggle as a lesbian growing up in a traditional, old-world, Romanian Orthodox family. She tried to marry a man to conform to the desires of her family members and found that it just felt wrong. Then she began to accept who she was and so did the rest of the family. I often tapped into my sister's past lives, fascinated by her karma. I saw her as a man in nineteenth-century Germany. A famous composer back then, she carried over into this life the love of women and the love of writing music. (She is also a wonderfully talented songwriter in this lifetime.)

On the other side, our souls know no gender. We tend to reincarnate again and again as the same gender, but sometimes our souls may switch genders in order to experience a different sort of life on earth or resolve outstanding karma. It all depends on what the soul needs to evolve, grow, and become complete. There are many cases in which an individual may not "feel right" in his or her body—these individuals feel that they should have been born the opposite sex. Some people actually undergo surgery to resolve this issue. This can be explained karmically as well: our souls have memory, and we might have a strong memory tied to us of being the opposite gender from past lifetimes. We might not feel comfortable in a certain body. Think about sleeping in the guest bedroom of someone's house. You're so used to your own bed that you may have trouble sleeping. Your body, mind, and spirit all possess strong memory.

Within any relationship, regardless of your gender or what gender you're attracted to, sex ebbs and flows. You have to be aware of what's becoming a habit and reflect on whether the amount and quality of sex you're having with your partner is working for you. When someone in a partnership has a low sex drive—so low that they're rarely having sex—there may be an underlying physical problem such as low levels of hormones. But usually, something psychological is going on. It could be that sexual abuse in your past is turning you off to sex—or making you promiscuous because you're trying to work out the karma that was created when you were abused. Emotional abuse related to sex can manifest in either direction. A client recently called me, Carmen, highly concerned about her adult son's inability to perform with a woman. "My son hasn't had sex in ten years," she cried. My client went on to explain that when her son was just twenty-two, his then-girlfriend constantly put him down, called him impotent, and said he wasn't a good enough sexual partner for her. This marked the man for life. Haunted by his awful ex-girlfriend's words, he became afraid to have sex with a woman. We all have what's called sexual pride—a sense of sexual security knowing we can perform intercourse well. Both men and women possess it. When someone demolishes your sexual pride, it can truly make you feel impotent or inadequate, unable to engage in an act that comes naturally to all human beings and is biologically necessary. As in the case of my client's son, psychological healing and therapy are needed to rebuild a healthy sense of sexual pride. Your soul may be calling to you to work through the pain of the past abuse, and having sexual problems can awaken you to this.

If sex with your partner is marked by controlling behavior, anger, or resentment, one or both of you may need counseling to get to the bottom of what's really going on. It may not be that you're no longer attracted to each other but that you have hidden issues affecting your sex drive. You see, sex is directly linked to our subconscious because it's uninhibited and untamed, as are the deeper levels of our mind. This explains why so many of our subconscious issues and tendencies may be manifested or become evident through sex. Freud was right when he said it all goes back to sexuality!

If you're out of touch with your body's pleasure, you need to get back in touch with it through your senses. You can return to the place where you and your partner fell in love, or do things you used to do together when you first paired up. Being in a physical space where you have powerful memories of being strongly attracted to each other can reignite passion. Or you can try something you've never tried before. The excitement of something new produces serotonin and dopamine in our brains. What's important is that you stop talking about taking that vacation, or trying that new spot, and follow through on your intention to reconnect with your partner.

If you have difficulty being monogamous, you have to be honest with yourself and your partner and decide how important it is to you to be faithful. Don't marry if you can't be faithful. This will only cause suffering and bad karma for you and your partner. Be true to who you are and don't pretend to be something you are not. Either go into a relationship fully or remain free to do as you please. And if your partner says he is not the monogamous type, believe him!

Relationships often get damaged by the pressures of the world outside the two people, whether it's the challenges of life or other people getting between you and distracting you from each other and your needs. The sex drive is very much influenced by stress. If you and your partner make a habit of checking in with each other and doing relationship maintenance, taking time to relax together and enjoy each other, you can prevent a relationship from falling apart. It's like doing regular maintenance on a car—you change the oil, brake pads, and other items to keep it running smoothly. Go too long without giving your car a checkup and you might find yourself calling AAA from the middle of the road. Don't postpone maintenance work on your relationship, or you may find yourself stranded on the side of the road . . . without your partner.

When you wake up, get dressed. Look sharp. It's too easy to let your looks go when you can count on your partner being there. Dress well and pay attention to your hygiene—and what the other finds attractive. Think as if you have to make your partner fall in love with you all over again each new day. Compliment each other regularly, for simple, sweet words can switch someone's mood instantly and restore much-needed confidence and self-esteem. Even if your partner has grown out of the habit of saying nice things to you, that doesn't mean you can't say them. Be the one who recharges your attraction to each other! Remember that the only way to help change someone else's behavior is by changing your own. If you begin to encourage your partner, the dynamic of your relationship will improve and your partner's behavior will change.

Two people in love should say three positive things to each other daily. This is unnatural to many because we're not taught about the importance of complimenting each other, but it really matters. Commit to establishing a new habit of doing this. The best compliment you can give to your partner is on something he or she cares about. If they treasure their work, tell them they're doing an amazing job. If they have an important meeting, wish them the best of luck before they rush out the door. If they've recently lost weight or changed their appearance, tell them they're beautiful. (There's nothing wrong with telling a man you love that he's beautiful, too!) Thank your partner for little things like bringing you a plate of food or putting something away for you. You tell complete strangers "thank you" for uncaringly holding a door open, so surely you can thank your partner for their constant time, commitment, and love. It's so ironic that sometimes we can thank just about anyone but our beloved. And we can say "I love you" with such ease to people who don't really matter, yet we choke on our words when saying it to the one person we really do love. Let's change this and put things, and people, into perspective. And of course, there is the mother of all compliments, one we would all love to hear from anyone at any given time because it deeply reassures us of our potential: "I'm proud of you." Hey, reader, I'm proud of you for your initiative to clear your karma and live an amazing life!

And don't criticize your partner in front of others. Brag about him or her, expressing pride. Never bring up personal details that might embarrass him, or talk about that time when he did something wrong or foolish, unless you know he enjoys being teased about it. In front of others, remember only the positive details.

Be affectionate and touch each other. Touch doesn't have to be about sex. A gentle caress on the arm or a tiny reach for your partner's hand can be absolutely enthralling. Don't underestimate the power of a tight embrace or a kiss on the forehead.

And take loving action. I, Carmen, was married to a man who wasn't demonstrative—many people aren't—but I saw his loving behavior. Loving action can mean getting your partner's tire pressure checked or setting up the coffee at night so you just have to press the button in the morning. Little sacrifices and small gestures that say "I'm thinking of you" make a big difference in maintaining your loving intimacy.

Whether your partner is your soul mate or a compromise, you'll still have to work to keep the love alive!

Balancing Intimacy and Separation within a Relationship

As with anything else in life, relationships must be balanced. *There is a time for everything and everything in time.* Our brains become resistant to dopamine over time, so that rush of excitement and the "butterflies in your stomach" diminish with repeated exposure. And if you or your partner travel often or are in a long-distance relationship, it will be more difficult to form that intimacy and familiarity that forms from living together or seeing each other regularly. The key to a lasting, loving, committed relationship is to balance time together and time apart. You have to give your partner a chance to miss you, a chance to "need" you close to him or her again. You also need a bit of time to yourself, to recharge and tend to your own needs and evaluate your next steps. As human beings, we were meant to be with others—but we were also meant to retain our individual identities and honor our alone time.

The way to recognize when you might need some time apart is to notice when tension or complacency begins to become evident in your relationship. If you and your partner are having trouble seeing eye to eye lately, or you routinely go through the day together with no romance or luster, it may be time to take a break.

This break doesn't have to last weeks or months, but it should be substantial enough to make you genuinely miss your partner. Maybe you can take a mini vacation by yourself or go visit your parents for a few days. During this time alone, reflect on your emotions and pay attention to what you're feeling when you think of your partner. If many negative emotions surface, further introspection may be needed to understand what's causing anger, bitterness, or frustration.

The tension and hard feelings may be caused by an energetic overload you receive from the other person. Recognize that you energetically affect each other. When you love someone, you take on that person's stress. When Virgil was sick, I, Carmen, didn't wear makeup and I gained thirty pounds. You actually carry weight when you're under stress, in part because you're probably not sleeping or eating well. In a situation like that, do your best to take care of yourself but be kind to yourself emotionally, too. And if one of you is anxious or angry, the other is going to be affected by the energy of those emotions, even if you're not actively fighting. A partner who is always irritable is going to affect you. It's okay to go off on your own and replenish yourself when your partner's angry, anxious, depressive, and so on. If you don't cleanse your energy, you run the risk of taking out pent-up irritations on your beloved, which can further strain a relationship.

Many people who have a birth code of 1 couple with other 1s. The problem is that 1s tend to have issues of independence and hardheadedness. So two 1s coming together will mean two partners who will spend a lot of time apart from each other. They will actually prefer to spend time apart rather than together. I, Carmen, had a mother, Sanda, who was a number 1. She displayed the usual tendencies of stubbornness and pride. My father, Victor, was a number 6, so he was quite the opposite from Sanda—silent, wise, and easily yielding. To my father, my mother was his life. But my mother wouldn't let herself get too comfortable or attached, even when they were together for more than forty years. She still kept her guard up and proudly showed her independence. Typical 1!

Sanda and Victor remained together until the very end, but Sanda's tendency to be too separate did at times add stress to the relationship. This strain would be particularly evident if two birth code 1s were to come together.

My husband, Virgil, also had a birth code of 1, which would explain why he didn't speak to me for an entire month one time after a minor argument. Thinking to leave for just a few days, I went down to Florida while he stayed in New York. Whether his independent personality made him need time away from his wife or his proud nature didn't let him call, I will admit that this time apart worked toward our benefit. He called me unexpectedly one day and said, "Come home," and I found myself on the next flight to New York, jittery with anticipation about seeing my husband whom I had seen a million times. He embraced me warmly when I walked through the door, and we were able to talk about our issues openly and honestly and plan a strategy so that the same argument wouldn't repeat again. Had we not taken a break (though I wish it hadn't been for so long!), perhaps we might not have come to a resolution so easily. My daughters have admitted to me that during the time that I was gone, he would ask them how I was several times a day.

Intimacy and separation both have their place in a relationship.

They must be balanced carefully to achieve the greatest dynamic possible between two people. If the energy is thrown off, a couple can easily fall apart—just as they can fall apart if the effects of love and time are not well understood.

The Dynamic of Love and Time

Love and time are two inseparable concepts. Love doesn't affect time, but time does affect love. No matter how much you love someone, time still passes by at the same rate. No matter how much you miss someone, time does not speed up. And no matter how much you just don't want to lose someone, time does not stand still. When Virgil was diagnosed with lung cancer, I, Carmen, remember thinking to myself, even praying, "God please, make time stop so I can have him here forever." But time continued in its usual way without any consideration for our family's happiness, and soon it was Virgil's time to go—something that neither I nor his daughters have completely accepted, although over time, the truth of his absence is sinking in our hearts as a ship sinks slowly to the bottom of the sea.

Whether we like to admit it or not, love allows itself to be affected by time. You can certainly still be in love with your partner after forty years of marriage, but I guarantee you it won't be the same kind of love as it was in your first four years together. You may still love your partner after a decade of being together, but excitement dwindles after a while and a kiss from him doesn't send you falling head over heels. Unfortunately, for most couples, love decreases or, even worse, completely dies out as time passes.

This happens because they don't work on the relationship, because they don't keep up with each other, and because they may simply be in a transitional relationship or a karmic one in which the karma has been resolved and no longer keeps them together. Time becomes a detrimental factor in these cases. But love can also build and become fortified with time.

The reasons for the fading of love are many, and can vary. Maybe one partner changes over time, someone needs change, the couple shares a loss they can't fully recover from, or a third person interferes in the relationship. Relationships all hit trouble spots, and it can be tricky to determine whether they can be saved.

Is it time for you to end the relationship? Stop for a moment and read the following list of words that describe a relationship still infused with love:

1. Excitement
2. Laughter
3. Energy
4. Willful sacrifice
5. Nurture

Are you excited when your partner walks through the door? Do you actually look forward to seeing this person at the end of the day? Do you laugh together and have energy for each other? Would you gladly sacrifice for the one you love? Do you enjoy nurturing and caring for your partner?

Now consider this list. Do these words resonate for you when you think about your relationship?

1. Blame
2. Judgment
3. Tired
4. Careless
5. Irritated

Do you blame your partner for things he or she has done wrong, or do you judge your partner for making decisions you feel are wrong? Do you feel emotionally, mentally, or physically tired around this person? Are you careless about your partner's needs, and prefer it if your partner just does everything alone, without your help or cooperation? Do your partner's mannerisms and habits irritate you much or all of the time?

Once you determine your own emotional standing, you can go on to evaluating your partner's, too. Ideally, you two will always be on the same page, whether both of you are in or out of love. If one of you is more in love than the other is, or if one of you is more loving and giving than the other, take action to make it right.

The two of us are firm believers in making things work. Divorce is always a valid option, but many times, people jump straight to it too quickly. This is not to say that if you've divorced, you've done anything wrong—absolutely not! But even if you are divorced now, maybe you want to discover some ways of keeping the love alive next time you find a great partner for you. And if you are presently in a relationship, work on your karma and work on your relationship. Don't abandon ship because you think it'll be easier. Listen to your instincts and be honest with yourself about how you are feeling. It is the only way to ensure that you will make the right choice about a relationship.

There are no "right" choices, but there are good and bad ones. Know that a relationship should nourish you. If it hasn't done that for a very long time, and your hard work on yourself and your relationship isn't producing the feelings of happiness, joy, and fulfillment you deserve, then it's time to consider whether you are ready to move on.

7

A CIRCLE OF FRIENDSHIP
THAT NEVER ENDS

(Unless You Resolve Your Mutual Karma!)

*What one doesn't know, the other can supply, and
what one hasn't yet experienced, the other can
explain. Such is the beauty of friendship.*

—ALEXANDRA HARRA

If you had to finish the sentence, "A friend is . . ." you would probably have a totally different answer than another person does, because friendship means something different to each of us. To some, a friend is a confidant, a person with whom to share your problems. To others, a friend is a person who will come to your rescue in an emergency. And to others, a friend is a buddy to spend time with and share laughter and fun moments. We create different definitions for friendship based on what we uniquely need from a person.

There's an old saying: "You can choose your friends but you

can't choose your family." Friends are an interesting category of relationships, because we do have a choice when it comes to the people we maintain as friends. Generally, we choose to associate ourselves with certain people because we either see moral value in them or share common interests with them. If our interests change or we enter a new stage of life, the friendship may not be as valuable to us as it once was.

When it comes to karma and friendships, some of our friends are people we knew in previous lives, which is why karmic ties with them can be very strong. In terms of family members, you recognize that you have an obligation of sorts, whether it's the duty to love your husband or care for your children or help your parents. Because of family bonds, you might have to maintain a reasonably friendly relationship with a relative you clash with because you don't want to create a family rift. But what obliges you to be so devoted to your friends? Are there karmic reasons for your being especially close to them?

Many of us don't realize that the close relationships we forge with others have their origins in past lives. Karmic relationships with friends are just as real as karmic relationships with lovers. There are telltale signs that your friendship is karmic in nature and you two have old stuff to work out. You may feel an instant connection when you first meet the person, or feel an inexplicable need to retain the friendship when others are saying, "I'm warning you—don't go near him. He's bad news!" or "Don't trust her. She has a lot of issues." In your spirit, you feel a deep need to be there for this friend despite the pleas for caution from others.

It's hard to say when you should cut a person off, set boundaries, or hang in there through the intensity. That decision is yours to make, although there are clear indications when to choose one route or the other. You might realize one day that it's simply the right time to let go, or you might end the friendship in a big dramatic moment. More often than not, people will feel confused and ambivalent and linger in a friendship that has become toxic. Just like remaining in a love relationship long after it's time to walk away, this can cause serious drawbacks in our own lives.

Lingering in a toxic friendship is often a sign that you need to work on your own issues so that you can more easily end the relationship and not be tempted to reengage the person and become hurt again. If you share bad karma with someone, you want to resolve it, not create more of it! And "hanging in there" when you're not supposed to only prolongs your and your friend's pain.

Your friends should be people you choose to love because your hearts connect. Sometimes, though, that connection is painful. It's when you know better than to maintain a particular friendship but somehow do it anyway that you can be sure there is a karmic element to the relationship.

The fact that you share karma with not just your romantic partners but also with your family and friends, neighbors, and coworkers can complicate your primary relationships, as we mentioned earlier. For example, a relationship with a close friend can interfere with your marriage, and your relationship with your sibling can affect your relationships with your parents. The intermingling of energies between relationships is to be expected. Friendships, however, should *not* become a burden. Friends are supposed to provide an escape from everyday worries. The time spent with them should be marked by laughter and joy, good conversation, and the more lighthearted elements of life. There are enough sorrows to attend to—your friends should not add to this. Romantic and family relationships can be painful enough, and jobs can be beyond stressful. If a friend is becoming a chronic burden, it's important to look honestly at the factors of that friendship.

Just like romantic relationships, friendships too can come into your life for only a limited period of time. And just as there are categories of romantic relationships, friends, too, come in three categories: teachers, distractors, and soul mates.

When friends act as teachers, they may be fulfilling a soul contract from the other side and may have come into our lives to guide us in learning a valuable lesson about change or self-betterment. Similarly, we may have to teach our friends valuable lessons in return—and it's possible we agreed to do this before we were born.

The best teachers can be friends who are at different ages or stages of life than we are. A lesson you learned about love at age eighteen, your friend may learn only at age thirty-two, and you can help guide her through it. A hardship regarding work might have provided valuable lessons and growth to your friend when she was in her twenties, and she can help you when you face something similar in your forties. This is where the beauty of friendship comes in: what one doesn't know, the other can supply, and what one hasn't yet experienced, the other can explain. Friends can give and receive unbiased, nonjudgmental guidance. And if they love us, they will do their best not to boss us around as they provide advice! But even the bossiest friends can mean well and be there for us at the most trying times, just as a beloved teacher might be extra hard on us because she knows we can rise to the challenge, but also be there to give us courage and faith in our-selves, coaching us along.

In the second category, friends who are distractors can be a lot of fun. They help us shift our mood when we're in painful circumstances. They are the ones who insist that we go out danc-ing when we are throwing a pity party for ourselves, and they're the ones who succeed in making us laugh when we want to scream in frustration. Their friendships are incredibly nourishing. Some-times, people choose to go on vacation with their friends following a particularly stressful season at work or a bad breakup because they know they need that infusion of good, positive energy. What a joy distractor friends can be!

You may not gain as much wisdom from your distractor friends as you do from your teacher friends, but they will play an important role in your life. Just be sure to know that not everyone can play both roles. A distractor may be insensitive when you are trying to confide in him or need thoughtful, wise advice. She may disappear on you when you're going through especially hard times. Having several distractor friends is helpful because you won't overburden them with your woes and moods. Understand that a distractor's role in your life is lighter than the other types of friendships and simply enjoy their amazing presence when they are there for you. Call on them when you know you need a break from frustration, grief, sadness, or anxiety, but don't expect them necessarily to be there under all conditions for you.

Lastly, friends can be soul mates, too. This type of soul mate is different from the romantic kind (although the two can blend—it is possible to fall in love with your best friend!). You know someone is a soul mate friend when you feel completely open with that person, able to tell him or her anything without fear of being judged or misinterpreted. As energy beings, soul mate friends vibrate at the same frequency we do. They are in sync with us energetically, and that's why they often share with us the same opinions as well as a powerful mental connection—that sort of "I was just going to call you and you beat me to it" bond.

Soul mate friends often meet each other during their childhood or teenage years and remain close throughout the entirety of their lives. Life circumstances such as distance, family, or duties may prevent soul mate friends from interacting as often as they would like, but as soon as they reconnect, it's as if no time has passed. They continue to share the same powerful bond, unchanged by time.

It's important to understand that what you may mean to a friend, they may not mean to you, and vice versa. I, Alexandra, have a soul mate friend named Arlene who is also my teacher. Arlene is the only person I feel comfortable asking for honest advice on the most sensitive matters. The friendship is mutual—Arlene is also unrestricted in sharing her concerns with me. I have another friend, Stephany, for whom I am definitely a teacher. But I see Stephany only as a distractor, and not a teacher in return. I can't share my troubles with Stephany for fear that she will judge me, as she has a habit of doing. So I gladly mentor Stephany but keep her at arm's length when it comes to divulging the more private matters of my life.

Understanding the roles of your friends can help you effectively navigate through your friendly relationships with ease and without drama, stress, or unnecessary discord. Know that all your friends will not play all three roles in your life. Distinguishing between the types of friends who come into your life will save you much disharmony and disappointment. You'll understand who you can and can't rely on, whom to seek if you need help, and who will jump into the role of best friend the moment she picks up the phone and sees your number. Discern the differences between them, but treasure all three types of friends.

Making New Friends

A common concern we hear from people is wanting to bring in new friends but not being able to. Many people say they feel stuck in the same dissatisfying friendships for many years but are afraid to let them go because they don't want to be friendless.

I, Alexandra, have a wonderful friend named Lauren. Lauren is sweet and mild-mannered, educated, and, unfortunately, completely unaware of her potential. I have observed for many years that Lauren seems stuck in a puddle of doubt. She is in the same job, the same types of painful relationships with romantic partners and unsupportive friends, but she just can't seem to find the courage or confidence to make changes. Lauren often confesses that she doesn't feel comfortable around her friends, and that she can't trust them with her secrets and can't ask them for advice because they tend to judge her. She says she'd rather stay in on a Saturday night than go out with her girlfriends, but then she forces herself to get dressed and go out with a crowd whose company she doesn't fully enjoy. When asked why she doesn't simply make some new, better friends, she claims her friendships feel comfortable in a way: she grew up with her friends or with people like them and is afraid she won't be able to make new friends if she lets go of the ones she has.

It is better to keep to yourself than force yourself to see people you don't love and who don't cherish you and your friendship. Lauren has become stuck in the cycle of allowing her simple distractor friends to take on the role of teacher friends or soul mate friends, and they just aren't up to it. This leads to much disappointment for Lauren.

Like most of us, Lauren has a subconscious fear of letting new people in. It may be that she doesn't feel capable of attracting new people or worthy of having friends who give her what she needs. Even if she does feel worthy, she doesn't know where to start or how to go about the challenge. But Lauren deserves to be surrounded by people who match her quality of being, and she will have to relinquish her fears in order to find them. And she's not alone. Many of us find ourselves in a similar predicament, unable to distance ourselves from people with whom we just don't click anymore and usher in new, more enlightened souls.

To welcome in new people, there are a few things we need to adjust within ourselves. We need to understand where the obstacles are: Are we afraid to make new friends, afraid of the work it involves, or are we just plain stuck in a comfort zone of the same energy for many years? What sort of energy do we give off? Is it warm and inviting or confrontational and closed off? Do we wear a smile on our face when we catch someone's eye, or a near frown because we've grown weary and cynical? To change friends we need to evaluate how we ourselves come across to others. Remember that we have to want to change and put in the appropriate action in order to enact change.

If you sometimes feel a bit closed off from others and find that you have trouble connecting but want to meet new friends who are in sync with you, practice this exercise for opening up and intermingling with different energies:

First, pick up a notebook or journal. Identify some of your most significant past friendships and answer the following questions:

How would you describe your former and current friends? What sorts of traits did they hold in common?

Were you often disappointed by their behavior and did you feel that you were putting more effort in than they were? If so, why did you hang on to those friends?

What qualities do you look for in your friends?

Are you okay with having a friend who is a teacher but not a soul mate or distractor? If you have had a friend like this, or still do, can you accept this friend's limitations?

Are you okay with having a friend who is a distractor but not a teacher? If you have such a friend, can you accept the limitations of the friendship?

Who are your soul mate friends? Write a bit about those friends and your relationships with them. Do they teach you? Inspire you? Distract you? Make you laugh? What are their qualities?

When you've finished writing, say a prayer of gratitude for each of your good friends. Tell yourself that you accept them exactly as they are. Imagine them being as happy as they make you!

It's imperative to recognize the quality of people you bring into your life. Seek people who vibrate at your frequency—that is, who share your values and are just as enlightened as you are, if not more so, when it comes to what matters most in life. We will open the doors of friendship to all sorts of questionable people, believing they can be changed or that they have a good heart and we should forgive them again and again for hurting us. At the end of the day, most everyone *does* have a good heart, but not everyone is worthy of your friendship and devotion. Be mindful of who you choose to spend time with and open your heart to. If you're serious-minded and have goals and aspirations, be careful about investing your heart in a friendship with someone who has none, is jealous of your accomplishments, or finds ways to nitpick your choices and values. A friend who can't be supportive of you and happy for you is not a friend you need. She can change your mood and energy and weigh you down. It's important to pay attention to how you feel—energized or drained, anxious or contented and happy—when you are around your friends.

The Energetic Nature of Friendships

Nature designed us as social creatures. We were meant to mingle, communicate constantly, and connect with each other on so many levels. It should come as no surprise, then, that in going about our everyday routines, we come into contact with hundreds of different energies: speaking with friends and family, listening to the many voices on TV, picking up tidbits of conversation from coworkers, and so on. Even asking the barista for your morning brew is a way of connecting!

Every energetic encounter, no matter how slight or fleeting, leaves an impression on our own field of energy. But what happens when we meet less-than-positive people and must interact with them and brew in their dark disposition? What happens when we continue to spend time with old friends who have become depressive, angry, or pessimistic? Their energies leave a stain on ours. Even a happy, upbeat person may soon find herself mimicking the negative behaviors of others because their energy has rubbed off on her.

First, we must learn to block out energies that are detrimental to our morale. Then it becomes easier to be a good, loyal friend and not end a friendship prematurely—but not become pulled into that friend's low vibrational frequency either. Here are six simple steps to banish bad energy from others and uplift your own energetic essence:

Step one: Identify any friends who are chronically anxious, irritable, sarcastic and snarky, or pessimistic and depressive. These friends might be under a lot of pressure, be going through a difficult time, or just have personalities that harbor darker, heavier emotions and lower a person's vibrational frequency. Some people simply see the glass as half empty rather than half full. That's fine for them, but their energy should not spill over onto you. Recognize friends who are "toxic" in nature and tread cautiously. They may be excellent teachers, but you do not want to adopt their low-vibrational energy.

Step two: Understand how your friends' moods affect you. Analyze how their negative energy is depriving your own state of being, your emotions, and your ability to function. Once you acknowledge the impact, you'll understand that their moods may be affecting you more than you think, leaving you physically and mentally drained. You may not realize it, but you absorb energies around you just as much as you absorb oxygen from the air.

Step three: Avoid maintaining friendships with people who give off bad energy. You should not have to "put up with" anyone's bad mood on a daily basis, whether the person is your boss, family member, or spouse. If you know someone who is constantly low-spirited due to life circumstances or otherwise, it might be time for you to politely create a bit of space between you. You can't run the other way whenever you see someone scowl, but you should shy away from people who emit chronic negativity and gravitate closer to those who praise a positive mind-set. Perhaps you're meant to be their teacher and guide them gently into getting help for depression and pessimism, but don't take on their karma. Tend to your own vibrational energy and mood.

Step four: Find a peaceful place to retreat to when someone else's energy is becoming toxic. In every friendship, there will be times when you need to find a place of solitude and spend some time there raising your vibrational frequency again before going back to interact with your friend. This space for retreat might be your private office, your bedroom, a bathroom, even your car. Retreat by not answering calls, texts, and instant messages if you need some space between you and a friend whose energy is too sour for you right now. The important thing is that you withdraw yourself from the unhealthy atmosphere and take a minute to recharge your own energy. When someone else's energy is making you feel uncomfortable, try affirmations. You can say things like, "I love myself, and therefore I protect my energy from the harmful vibes of others."

Step five: Create an energy shield of protection. Your energetic territory is your very own personal space of being, and few people should have access to this private part of yourself. If you're an open person who invites others into your "energy bubble," you grant them the opportunity to modify your mood and mold your well-being to their liking. Remember that when someone enters your energy field, their own state of being doesn't trail far behind. If you feel this happens to you often, keep your energetic doors closed to invaders. Visualize a bubble of protection enclosing you safely when you feel your emotional space is being invaded. If a friend invades your space regularly, you need to confront that person and set a clear boundary.

Step six: Keep your own emotions in check. We often believe we don't have the power to control our emotions, but we do! To maintain healthy friendships, we all need to improve our ability to manage our feelings of anger, jealousy, sadness, and so on. Otherwise, we will overburden our friends, lower our vibrational frequency, and begin to attract people who are of a lower frequency and who often display darker emotions.

Take control of your negative emotions before they take control of you. The worst mistakes are made in moments of anger, which raises adrenaline levels and causes people not to see straight. The more you enable anger, the more the nerve cells of your brain evoke this emotion. Similarly, the more you practice feelings of tranquillity, unconditional love, and joy, the more easily and frequently you will slip naturally into these moods, raising your vibrational frequency and attracting others who are at your level of emotional well-being.

Take these six simple steps into consideration the next time you connect to the energies of others—that might be very soon!

ALEXANDRA

Business and Pleasure, and Complications

The old saying goes "Never mix business with pleasure." Another is "Never mix business with family." But in my case, that's plain unavoidable. I love my mom and have worked with her since I was in high school.

The truth is that we work perfectly together. We're not just mother and daughter—we're soul mate friends. But a challenge we face is that my mother is a magnet for people who drain her of her energy—not in terms of her work, though she does work with her energy, but in terms of people who wheedle their way into her life to suck from her love and/or resources.

I can remember the only time I literally kicked someone out of our house—yes, I planted my stiletto heel on someone's butt! Believe me, it was much deserved. You see, several years ago, my mother approached me with the idea of bringing in another assistant to help her manage her company. I immediately furrowed my eyebrows in dismay, as I had held the position for as long as I could remember. But her point was valid: the business was expanding, and she did need someone to coordinate the European clients, as I focused much more on the American side. I reluctantly agreed, sensing something not-so-great was bound to happen. (Yes, my own intuition is very highly developed.)

A redheaded, thirty-year-old woman named Dora walked into our home, jittery with excitement at the opportunity to work with Dr. Harra. I eyed her as an unfriendly cat eyes the new family dog. But I tolerated her until I started seeing unpleasant signs. Dora was asking for just a bit much from my vulnerable and ever-loving mother. First, she took over our vacant apartment a few blocks away from the house—not as an office but as a home. And I thought, fine, I'll allow it for a couple of months until she gets on her feet. A couple of months turned into half a year, at which point Dora was already decorating the place to her liking. She came to our home every morning and fixed herself breakfast, and then soon she was fixing herself lunch, too, and then she was scrounging around the refrigerator to make herself some dinner—on a regular basis. My mother bought Dora clothes and shoes and all the things she said she needed—this on top of Dora receiving a respectable salary given the work she was doing. Dora sat in front of the computer day and night, claiming to be working on my mother's social media and client e-mails, though not much ever got done. All the while, my mother was insisting that Dora was a wonderful friend, and how lucky we were to have her help-ing us out. Despite how much I dyed my hair, I was getting gray hairs from the stress of this invader.

I reached my breaking point when Dora came up with the idea that European clients who didn't have credit cards and needed to pay for their sessions through Western Union should send the money directly to her. This method, she claimed, would save my mom precious time in not having to go down to the West-ern Union office to collect the payments. Dora would, of course, give the money to my mom once she collected it, and she would schedule the clients once the money was received.

Do you see where this is going?

Unfortunately, my mom didn't. Whatever concerns I raised, she dismissed. (Not to rub it in, but . . .)

A week later, a European client forwarded me an e-mail she had written to Dora. In it, she complained about never having been scheduled to speak with Dr. Harra, though she had sent the money via Western Union. I asked Dora about this, and she claimed that the client was delusional and of course she had been scheduled for her session. But I smelled that something was off. I took a look at Dora's e-mails while she was away and caught a number of clients complaining about not having been scheduled, although they had sent the money by Western Union under Do-ra's name. I also found several Skype conversations between Dora and a certain gentleman in which she described Carmen and me in less-than-polite terms. I had seen enough. I ambled into the office, where my mom and Dora were conversing, gently gripped Dora by the arm, and escorted her to the front door. And when she protested, I admit, the sole of my shoe met her rather generous bottom.

Why was my mother, a gifted intuitive, so blind to Dora's treachery? Love, compassion, and kindness—and a schedule so busy she didn't sit down and listen to her instincts. (My mother would say that I can be just as bad as she is when it comes to getting caught up in extending love to undeserving people . . . er . . . gentlemen.) In terms of mixing family/friends and business, pay close attention: you may be extra sensitive to a person because you've grown attached to them, and therefore your emotions won't let you see their wrong intentions or actions, which are hindering your business. Regard them, for a minute, as a stranger: do you see now what they're doing wrong?

Perhaps you work with a circle of friends or coworkers, or volunteers, and see that while everyone worked together beautifully at first, some people have become bossy, unreliable, or difficult. These sorts of changes are hard to avoid because as trust builds, people's true colors begin to show. If you're the boss, remember that you are helping them learn karmic lessons when you tell them to pull it together or move on! If you are not the boss, the best thing you can do when coworkers and business partners start to take advantage of you or shirk their responsibilities is to perform your own portion of the work and leave them to their jobs. Do not cover for them—bring the problems to your boss's attention, without creating unnecessary drama. Step back and protect your heart if you're really there for the work or the cause.

If you see that someone is standoffish or nonresponsive to a good work relationship with you, or if she doesn't take your gentle hints and requests to change her behavior toward you, there is only so much you can do. If it's a work situation, be aware that you may be the one who gets in trouble for your coworker's lack of attendance to her work if you don't speak up. You may have to rescue a project if some volunteer is always promising to do this or that and never follows through and your boss is not there to deal with the issues. Stand up for yourself, but try as much as possible to keep the drama out of these situations. Do what you do, with passion. Do excellent work. Follow through on your commitments. Engage everyone in the circle of workplace community and be cordial but somewhat distant to the one who is bringing in negative energy. Don't reply to them in nasty or standoffish ways, as this can turn ugly quickly, and you don't want to stoop to their level.

Withdraw yourself from negative situations with friends, coworkers, and others in your community. The secret of truly successful people is that they keep to themselves when the drama gets going. They work for themselves, by themselves. They leave the pettiness behind them as they climb upward. They thrive on their own creativity and put energy into productive friendships and partnerships that nourish people and avoid lowering themselves into the ugliness of dramas.

Friends Can Save Your Life!

Studies show that socializing increases our life span and improves our mood and overall health. There is a direct link between spending quality time with others and feeling better on an emotional, mental, and physical level. Isolation and solidarity, on the other hand, can lead to depression and anxiety. Being a social butterfly and having plenty of good friendships is truly beneficial to our health. If we are smart enough to seek friends of a like mind and quality and we're wise enough to accept others as they are, we can enjoy positive, enriching relationships with all sorts of people. Then we may even live longer, happier lives.

Try to have a variety of friends. Treasure their insights and different experiences that can teach you golden lessons. While you should always try to pair up with people as evolved as you are, you should also seek people of various walks of life. Have friends of different ethnic backgrounds, or of the opposite gender. Have friends of different sexual orientations, or who are older or younger than you are. I, Alexandra, believe that my generation—as intelligent and goal-oriented as it is—can teach me a lot, but only by associating with people of different ages can I tap into a true fountain of wisdom. While she was alive, my grandmother was my best friend. There is no wisdom like that of the elder who's already walked down the roads that await us all. In this way, I can gain the precious knowledge held by all of us collectively. I have learned the secrets of a long and happy marriage from my eighty-four-year-old next-door neighbor, who was married for more than sixty years. No self-help book, audiotape, or online program can divulge such wisdom (although our book, I would say, comes close).

We can evolve by listening to the accounts of others and absorbing the colorful episodes they've lived through. This helps us better understand how to approach our own challenges of life.

Our knowledge begins to expand when we hear as many voices as possible and supplement what we don't yet know with what the experiences of others can teach us.

But increased exposure to others who aren't always of a like mind can also easily increase tensions. We all know how difficult it is to maintain cordial relationships at all times, so how can we keep our friendships free of drama? Refer to the list in Chapter 5 about how to maintain peaceful relationships that have healthy boundaries. Keep in mind, too, that friendship bonds may fray if you take them for granted. People often feel a stronger loyalty to family and put more effort into relationships with those to whom they are related. Do not neglect your friendships, however, thinking that since you have been friends with a person for a long time, you can take that person for granted! This will inevitably set up bad karma for you.

Communication: The Key to Friendship

The key in any relationship is good communication. This includes not making assumptions about others, not taking things personally when it's likely they're not meant personally, and clarifying what the other person feels toward you. Clear communication lies at the heart of human interaction. Don't say you're letting your frustrations with your friends roll off your back when you aren't. Speak up! If you can't express your emotions, concerns, and honest thoughts, your friendship won't be sustainable. Arguments, conflicts, misunderstandings, and hurt feelings are a part of any friendship—but they can be rare and mild if avid communication is present.

Let's say you just had a ruthless argument with your best friend. Now what? Compelling communication is especially tricky in friendships because of the high level of the ego on both sides. Letting your friend know your true intentions and lessening your ego are both essential elements in reaching a resolution. Tell your friend that although you don't agree with him, you're still supportive and would like to discuss what happened. The voice of communication in a friendship is dependability and selflessness.

Isn't it funny that there are over a million words in the English language but so many of us still have trouble getting our point across to others? Our emotions overwhelm us, insecurities tie our tongues down, and mental filters restrict us from speaking the contents of our hearts. Our self-imposed limitations result in a loss for words or the wrong words coming out altogether. It's genuinely difficult to confess our innermost thoughts and feelings with no bounds, and this is why we all encounter communication barriers in one form or another. Yet if we can communicate effectively, we can enrich all our relationships.

Speak to someone as you would have her speak to you. If you must bring up a sensitive issue, ask yourself, "How would I want someone to bring it up if it were me having this problem?" Turn the situation toward yourself and you'll find the right way to say it. By choosing to communicate in a loving, respectful, yet honest way, you truly will ensure golden friendships that can last a lifetime.

8

WHAT DOESN'T KILL YOU MAKES YOU STRONGER

(And Wiser!)

*There is no death and no loss. There is only
the mind that reaches heaven.*

—DR. CARMEN HARRA

Even when our relationships are strained, losing them because of a death is devastating. The lack of closure—the inability to make things right before our time together on this earth ends—can haunt us. However, if you knew what we know about the invisible realm, you would take much comfort in knowing that death does not have to end a relationship. It only changes the nature of a relationship, sometimes in positive ways, believe it or not. The bonds of a heartfelt connection between two people can't be severed by the departure of a soul from a body!

You see, while there is a physical world, the one we experience with the five senses each day, there is also a divine world, a realm where time and earthly matters are nonexistent. In the physical world, our ancient souls have taken on the temporary form of human bodies, and we go about our everyday rounds trying to achieve whatever it is we have put our minds to. But in the divine world, there is no pain, no daily pressures, no burden, and no loss. There is no grieving on the other side, because all souls are together. If a soul wants to check in on a soul that's temporarily taking human form, it can do so easily. Souls on the other side don't feel the disconnection from us that we feel from them. They are here, perhaps sitting in their favorite chair in the living room, unbeknownst to us, surveying us lovingly. Our loved ones' physical deaths may shatter us, but on the other side, they don't feel the loss. They actually feel much better than they did here, unburdened and without worries.

Loss, the root of all grief, is the human-made notion that someone we love has left our life. But there is no such thing. All loss is temporary. It's the higher realm where we reunite after we pass on that is permanent.

A higher understanding of our interconnectedness in this life and in the realm where we exist before we're born helps us accept our losses whether they are death or breakups. That we are always connected to those we love is not a false panacea for grief offered by religion. It is a spiritual truth. And that we will reunite with our dear departed is an inevitability.

Most of our meetings on earth are predestined—we were born into our family and make the special connections we make because they were written in our soul's contract. Our spirit agreed to complete certain missions on earth before it reincarnated into a body, and these missions are our individual karma we must fulfill. Our greatest purpose, however, is to fulfill our outstanding karma without creating any more negative karma. Otherwise, we will have to repeat this physical life time and time again until our karma is resolved. The next time you want to run away from your karma with a person you don't particularly like, think about this: either you can put in a bit of effort to resolve your karma with this person during this lifetime, and never have to come in contact with them in the future, or you can avoid doing the work now and have to put up with them again and again in your following lifetimes. Which would you rather have? Do your work now.

Many of us can relate to taking care of a loved one toward the end of that person's life on earth. Whether it was our parent, spouse, family member, friend, or even our child, we all know how excruciating the process of passing can be, both for our loved one and also for us. In those last days, our beloved may not even resemble himself or herself. Medications, dementia, and comas may cause a person to be inactive, immobile, and helpless. Our loved ones may be unresponsive, unable to think or speak clearly, and lacking the unique spirit and vitality that we loved so much about them. Their personalities change, and they seem to have no personality as they lie in a hospital bed. For family and friends, it's heart-wrenching. Yet we can take some comfort in knowing that what we are experiencing is very different from what they are experiencing.

The process in which a person is "between the worlds" before they pass is called *dementia*. It's a temporary state in which a soul is able to leave the body and return to it while a person is still alive. On the one hand, the body is fighting to stay alive. On the other hand, the soul wants to break free and can do so temporarily. This is why so many people who are terminally ill just don't act like themselves anymore: their perceptions may have shifted dramatically. Often, they can't express themselves, which is frustrating for them when they become aware of the disconnection between what's going on inside them and what they're able to express. With dementia, a gentle person can become chronically angry and short-tempered, while an aggressive and belligerent person can become sweet and docile. It can be very difficult emotionally to handle the changes you observe in a person at the end of life.

Even up to the very end, there can be moments where there's a quick return to life: the spirit comes back into the body, and the person is inexplicably back, if only for a minute or two, speaking like he or she always did, making the same hand gestures and processing thoughts normally. These abilities are fleeting, but they give you a glimpse of the person you knew and loved. I, Carmen, remember going through this stage—in which the soul enters and leaves the body—with both my mother and my husband. In her last days, my mother fell into a coma, so her spirit was pretty much gone from this world. But before that, Sanda would alternate between asking me whether I had cleaned the house and washed the dishes before coming to see her and hardly being able to whisper a yes or no in response to questions. It was the same thing with Virgil, who would go from joking around with the nurses and asking them to put a drop of vodka in his IV (typical of his sense of humor!) and being unable to open his eyes to look at his family as we crowded around his bedside—all in a matter of seconds.

Anyone who has experienced the loss of a loved one can relate to these last moments in which a spirit enters dementia. The comfort is in knowing that the person experiences freedom when the spirit finally crosses over. Then they are no longer weighed down by the burdens of the physical world and have been liberated from their suffering. This is when we begin a new kind of relationship with the person—a different kind of connection that is equally strong as was our connection to them in the physical world. In fact, our connection to a spirit in the other realm can be stronger than it was when the person was alive, if we work to solidify that connection. What feels like it's going to kill us—a loss so great we can barely wrap our minds around it—can in fact make us much stronger and open the doors to communication with the divine world.

Grief and Karma

Knowing when to let go of our emotions and how to release them so that we can manage our grief can be an incredible challenge. After a loss, we're told "take time to grieve," but not how to accomplish that! Is there a correct way to grieve, one that allows us to pour forth our negative emotions more efficiently so that they don't become trapped in our being?

Without a doubt, grief, fear, and anger can be destructive, but they can also bring us closer to each other and to God. We want the latter, of course. The only way to turn the grieving process into a bonding process is to release our emotions in ways that are healthy. Too often, we lash out at those around us. Our rage about our loss comes out as yelling at nurses or snapping at well-meaning friends who just came to visit.

The problem is that we seldom release emotions the way we should. We naturally think it's better to keep them bottled inside us, assuming that there they'll diminish and eventually disappear. If only! On the contrary, emotions that are bottled up will do two things: first, they'll boil within our being, mounting in force and power and eating away at our health, and second, they'll erupt at the wrong time and with the wrong person. Far worse than taking out your multiplied anger on someone who doesn't deserve it is the fact that emotions can cause us to become stuck with unwanted karma. An emotion is, believe it or not, a living thing, because it's attached to a living thing (you). It is a brain response being carried out within a real person. Emotions and you have memory: you remember what it's like to be angry, and anger remembers what makes you most angry. Emotions that remain trapped inside become attached to your memory and your being. They become fused with your already existing karma, adding on to it. That's because karma is the memory that's weighed down and preserved by emotion.

And karma—memory cluttered with emotion—can be passed down from parent to child, or transferred within the family, since all karma is shared. It can continue to manifest in your life over and over again until it's carried over into the next life. Virgil's mother died when he was in his twenties, hit by a vehicle as she was crossing the street. Stricken by shock and grief, he never processed his emotions and they remained bitterly blocked within him. They seem to have manifested into his karma, however, because he died young as well.

I, Alexandra, lost my father in my early twenties to lung cancer from smoking cigarettes, a habit he picked up just after his mother died. Now I will have to work extra hard not only to break the karma by releasing the grief but also to replace it with positive emotions and actions. I realize that distracting myself from my emotional discomfort is healthy here and there—you can't experience sadness every moment—but I also know how important it is to process my emotions thoroughly and release them.

I'm determined not to get stuck with the family karma, which is why I supplement thought with action, a necessary step in breaking karmic cycles. My father smoked to mask his mismanaged grief caused by losing his mother, but I abhor cigarettes. My dad would turn and hide within himself because of this buried grief, and although I share the same tendency, I'm learning to open up and share my problems with my ever-supportive family. My father was stubborn to the point that he refused to see a doctor even when he was coughing up blood, and I was born with the same stubborn nature. But when it comes to my health, I've learned the hard way not to think I know best, and I get regular checkups to make sure I'm healthy.

I'm also learning to release raw emotions for the sake of keeping my karma clean. Otherwise, I acknowledge that my future will become weighed down by it. For example, I met a lovely girl in college who had recently lost her father. Being twenty-six and utterly demoralized, she soon found comfort in a man in his fifties. Interestingly enough, this girl continued to deny that she had any "daddy issues." And this is typical: a woman who has lost a father when she was young may be attracted to an older romantic partner who is like a father figure for her. She might overlook flaws in such a man because of a deep yearning to replace the father she lost. Knowing that, I am committed to releasing my grief over my father and resolving the karma created by his death instead of surrendering to its karmic implications.

CARMEN

The Grief That Can Overwhelm You

You must let out raw emotions after a loss so that you don't feel overwhelmed and you don't overwhelm your loved ones. After my husband's passing, I needed extra support from the family. I was admittedly weak, afraid, and anxious. Like so many others who have lost a spouse, I found myself waking up in the middle of the night sweating and reaching over to the other side of the bed for Virgil. I often thought of the lines "Tears of the widower, when he sees / A late-lost form that sleep reveals, / And moves his doubtful arms, and feels / Her place is empty, fall like these," written by Alfred, Lord Tennyson in *In Memoriam*, his book-length poem about grief and loss. Virgil's absence, especially following an all-too-vivid dream in which he was present, was a grim reality to wake up to.

My emotions—fear, anger, grief—were constantly churning and flowing through me. I was anxious and in pain, and I found it hard to prevent my emotions from spilling out onto the other family members. I called my stepdaughters over more often than ever. I visited Virgil's other family members to the point that I felt as if I were intruding. I pestered Alexandra nonstop over little things that were stressing me out in my state of vulnerability and woundedness. I realized that everyone was making slow, steady progress . . . except me.

After a bit of careful reflection, I came to understand the reason behind that: I wasn't releasing my raw emotions. I was trying to put on a strong face for everyone, yet I was crumbling inside. I would release bits and pieces of these emotions, at the wrong times and in the wrong ways, like weeping in the bread aisle of the supermarket or yelling at my grandchild for innocently spilling something on the floor. Repressed grief leads a person to lash out at others, or avoid connecting with someone who cares. Bad karma gets created—and makes matters worse. I had to make a commitment to releasing my grief so as not to be overwhelmed and shut down altogether.

Several years ago, I had a client named Albert. Albert's main concern was being unable to overcome the passing of his wife of many years. When I asked him how he handled her loss, he confessed that he mostly stayed in his house for months and didn't really reach out to people, not even his children. Now, years later, Albert felt ready to date again but didn't even know where to start. He said he tried to go out at times and speak to women, but the conversations always felt meaningless and he quickly lost interest. Albert said that it felt like there was a void in his heart that couldn't be filled with anything. Indeed, he had created a very bitter, lonely karma for himself. His connection with his kids wasn't the same, and he simply lost interest in pursuing a joyful life. Albert's locked-up grief had turned into depression because he never released it. This is a situation all of us must avoid even as we can't avoid devastating loss.

Grief Release

It's not fair to ourselves to allow our emotions to sabotage our potential of being happy. It's not fair to ourselves or the people who love us to allow grief and suffering to become permanent fixtures of everyday life. Why succumb to this when it's possible to pull yourself to the surface of the water and discover the bright sky overhead? Time doesn't always heal all wounds. You have to release your emotions so that your wounds can heal and become scars that fade. It's not easy to tolerate the pain of raw emotions, but just a little bit of "grief release" each day eventually leads to the resolution of karma.

It is extremely difficult to fill a soulful abyss after losing a spouse, child, parent, sibling, or friend, or after suffering several losses back-to-back. Fortunately, we come equipped with the most wonderful grace imaginable: resilience. Fortitude and endurance, getting up and forging ahead, allow us to conquer almost anything. Profound resilience never fails to see us through. And knowing this is the first step toward true healing after loss.

Several strategies are very effective for releasing negative emotions within you and freeing your spirit from lingering anguish.

The first is journaling. If you're a man, please don't think that only women write in journals. You don't have to get a pink journal with butterflies on it! (Although it would definitely be a conversation starter with the ladies.) You can write in a notebook that feels comfortable for you to own and work with daily. Many creative people have journaled in notebooks, including film directors, great artists such as Leonardo da Vinci, and even Steve Jobs. The idea is to write about your thoughts, ideas, and feelings, or simply to draw them. This allows you to access your emotions and find an outlet for them. Do not be afraid to cry! Crying energetically releases emotions. If you're embarrassed to cry in front of others, then make a point of being alone at times so that you can journal about your feelings and allow the tears to flow. And keep in mind that unlike just speaking or thinking about your emotions, writing them down makes them tangible—the writing process helps you acknowledge the value of your feelings. Men and boys too often are told not to cry or be sentimental or sensitive and forget how to feel, but repressing emotions can lead to creating bad karma inadvertently. Let yourself feel and even cry as you write. You can revisit the pages later, when you feel much better, and congratulate yourself for having triumphed over your grief at the time by not fearing its power—and by containing it, writing about it in a journal that you are able to set aside whenever you decide, "That's enough for now."

The second strategy for grief release is to develop a strong support system. Spend time with whoever offers you moral support and makes you feel comfortable expressing your emotions or setting them aside when it feels right to engage in activities you enjoy. You might find that your strongest allies at this time are best friends or family members. However, they could be people who have come into your life recently—through a support group, or through the "coincidence" of meeting you at a time when you are both recovering from loss. (Coincidences are actually synchronicities—events that are meant to happen.) Stick closely with those who can boost your strength and vitality, and don't be afraid to call on people who can show you unconditional love and patience in a time when you need compassion above all else. By surrounding yourself with support, you make it easier for yourself to feel and express the grief that can seem frightening because of its intensity. Knowing that you are okay—that you can break down and cry and there will be someone to pick up the slack and get a meal on the table, get work done, and watch your children, is incredibly helpful when you need to take time to grieve.

The third strategy for releasing raw emotions is to tame your grief by putting limits on it. Cry, and allow yourself to feel angry and resentful that you've suffered a terrible loss. Don't temper your emotions, but do express them without letting them overtake you for hours or days. If you need a good cry, hop in the shower and cry for ten minutes. Write three pages in your journal, filling it with your emotions even as your tears fall on the page, and then close it for the day. Or take a walk in nature in a secluded area and just let everything out while you are there, and then take a deep breath as you exit the path that wound through the woods. Go to a lake or ocean and throw rocks into the water, or cry as you float on its surface for a time. Don't hold back the torrent of feelings, but set out with the intention of having the emotions stop when the activity stops. When you put a time limit on your grief, you're not grieving constantly, which is important, as that comes with the danger of embedding your grief into your being and creating a permanent niche for it to return every day.

Affirmations after a Loss

Recite these ten affirmations to steady your emotions and uplift your spirits during trying times:

> *My pain is momentary. It will not span into my future.*
> *This situation is teaching me a necessary lesson.*
> *Through this hard time, I am learning and evolving.*
> *I have the power to turn this setback into a victory.*
> *My path is clear. I know exactly what I must do.*
> *I am sustained by people who support me through anything.*
> *My suffering is heard. I will be rewarded with pure joy.*
> *I will resurface after this storm, stronger and better than before.*
> *Determination and ambition surge through me.*
> *An unexpected blessing awaits me.*

When you say these affirmations, allow yourself to feel them fully. Say them until you can say them with faith and conviction. It can take a few repetitions to create optimistic feelings, but when you do, you actually change your vibration and send a message to the universe that you are ready for these statements to be true not just in your mind but in your life.

ALEXANDRA

....

"Out of Difficulties Come Miracles"

I can conjure three distinct memories from my childhood and teenage years in Queens, New York, where I grew up: the strong smell of my father's cooking wafting underneath my bedroom door; the long-awaited coming of spring and with it, the blooming of the old tree in our backyard and laughter of the neighborhood kids playing outside; and last, a plaque on my wall that read: "Out of difficulties come miracles."

I was a child who, fortunately, didn't have many difficulties to undergo. My mother and father took them on for me. Financial matters, family problems—they weren't mine to worry about. So I was lucky enough to concern myself with my schoolwork, friends, and trends of the moment as typical children do. But every day, I looked at the plaque and read those words festooned with flowers: "Out of difficulties come miracles." I read that plaque as I entered my room, and at night as I dozed off to sleep, and in the morning when it caught my eye briefly.

"Out of difficulties come miracles" became somewhat of a motto for me, like a song you hear over and over again on the radio that gets stuck in your head. But I didn't fully comprehend just what miracles could come out of difficulties, for I had next to no pain in my life. It wasn't until my father passed that I experienced a head-on collision with a big difficulty. And what then?

What miracle could possibly come out of my father's passing? The grief echoed constantly throughout the chambers of my being. My plaque, the one item in my house I most concentrated on for years without even realizing it, had taunted me with a downright lie. When it came time to clean out my father's closet and gently dispose of his belongings, the plaque went right with them. I remember feeling disgust at the broken promise of my pretty plaque as I shoved it into a garbage bag.

Perhaps a year passed without me repeating that phrase in my mind. My mom and I locked up the house in Queens quite suddenly and moved to Florida with our pets (I temporarily lost Valentino, the family dog, during the trip, as you read in Chapter 6).

Christmas was coming and we were distraught—and dizzy from the faint scent of my father on his old belongings. I didn't visit New York for a while—the pain was still too fresh. Finally, I decided to come up to our Queens home for a few weeks. Unlocking the house and entering after so many months felt like stepping into an abandoned castle. There were my father's prized paintings he had collected over a lifetime, glittering all over the walls—the bronze statues and porcelain figurines and antique furniture. What a skilled art dealer he had been! I appreciated them for a moment, beholding the strange relics I once took to be ordinary objects in my house. I walked upstairs and into my room. Everything was as I had left it last year, collecting dust . . . everything but the plaque.

Spotting that empty space on the wall, I felt a surge of emotion. I needed to find not the plaque, but its meaning. I needed to believe that out of difficulties could indeed come miracles. But where to begin walking what seemed like an ever-winding road?

I started with the first place to reconnect with my loss: my father's grave. This was the first time I would visit since the burial and, granted, I felt a little awkward going into a cemetery by myself. It took me nearly two hours to find the grave—none of the family members could explain how to get to it. My half sister said it was by the "big old tree," which wasn't much help because the cemetery was laden with big old trees. My mother told me to go down to the end and then make a left. She didn't seem to remember that the cemetery was sprawled out in a circle! The main office couldn't locate the grave (a slight misspelling of the last name in their records was the problem). I scoured this place of the dead, walking past endless tombs, flowers in hand beginning to wilt, until I finally came upon my beloved father's grave. I collapsed on the grass and laid the flowers by the headstone.

I wasn't sure where to start, so I simply began speaking as if he were there, as I used to speak to him every afternoon when I got home from school. I released my frustrations, anger, wishes, and desires to him. I asked him why he left, and how could he leave my mom all alone. I was mad and I told him so, crazy though it might sound. I could always talk to my dad honestly, so I wasn't going to stop now.

I reminded him that he always promised us he would live to be a hundred years old. I laughed as I recounted that he thought he'd outlive all of us. It was strangely comforting, because I realized he was listening.

I soon moved back to New York for various reasons. I was no longer afraid to be in a place that held so much pain, because that pain had been replaced by hope. Twice a week, I made it a habit to visit my father's grave, lay flowers, and sit and talk. I did not miss one opportunity to go to him, whether it was snowing or raining. It became almost my secret hiding place, my few minutes a few times a week to retreat and regain tranquillity and faith. I took comfort in our little talks, and although he didn't speak back to me, I could figuratively hear his voice in my mind, guiding me and giving me advice from the other side. I came to understand that although I don't think it was his time, perhaps my father chose to go—in part to avoid the suffering and misery of his illness, but also so that he could help us in unimaginable ways from beyond. He's given us incredible aid that he could have never given us if he were here on earth. Certainly we have felt his divine help on more than one occasion. I don't believe without his help I would be fulfilling my life's dream of writing a book. I don't believe without his help we would have been granted a television show. And there are many, many other things I know he's had a divine hand in bringing about.

When I was little, I somehow knew that the message of that plaque would bloom into full meaning one day. I came to understand that out of difficulties actually emerge not one, but five, miracles: the miracle of resilience, because we are able to spring back from any trouble; the miracle of awareness, because our woes really open our eyes to reality; the miracle of unity, because human souls seek each other when we are suffering; the miracle of a new chapter, because loss signifies the end of a painful ordeal; and the miracle of unexpected help, because from the other side, our loved one's aid becomes infinite. We can overlook these miracles as though they were ordinary elements of life, or we can take them as the proof that Spirit grants us just what we need in our worst moments. I took them as the latter.

Three Lessons in Overcoming Loss

The impact of loss is heavily influenced by the way we think. Having the right mind-set can help you cope with the pain. If you think that the deceased person is no longer suffering on earth and it's possible to maintain a solid connection with them on the other side, the loss will be ameliorated. But if you become trapped in suffering, pain will be prolonged and deepened if you don't make an effort to alter your thoughts.

And you can choose your thoughts. Consider the following three strategies to regain a sense of inner security and overcome your challenges after loss.

Strategy 1: See beyond the moment.

Seeing beyond a moment in time and to a better future that doesn't exist yet is difficult, but future projection is our saving grace during misfortune. You may hurt today, and deeply, but the pain will subside in time. If you shift your thoughts away from, "Why did this happen?" to "What lesson can I learn from this to make the loss more tolerable and make it lead to a change for the better?," your agony will be alleviated. See every obstacle as an opportunity for personal growth. Close your eyes and take a deep breath. Allow reality to set in and open yourself up to the lesson. It may not come to you the first time you "meditate on" what can be learned, but if you keep reminding yourself that good can come out of the worst tragedies, you will stay open to the opportunity to learn and grow. When you look past the grief you're experiencing in the moment, you can regain hope—hope that "this too, in time, will pass," hope that happiness will return, and hope that you will begin and lead a brand-new chapter of life that can be filled with insurmountable joy.

Strategy 2: Take positive action.

Although nothing can replace what you've lost, taking any action, no matter how small, to create or bring about something new can help usher you out of grief. If you've recently lost your partner, take time to rediscover your personal needs and devote time to activities you enjoy on your own. Get out and meet new people by taking a class or joining a group or attending an event. Force yourself. Even if you don't have a great time, reward yourself and praise yourself for having made an effort to rise above your sadness for just a few hours.

Strategy 3: Change and redirect.

After a loss, changing your circumstances may be the best way to overcome your heartache. Don't be afraid to make major life shifts after misfortune has hit. Maybe you've always wanted to move, and now might be the perfect time. Pack up your things and go—don't be afraid to take a leap of faith and act on what you've wanted to act on for a long time. Apply for that new job, redecorate your home, trade in the car you shared with your partner, and so on. Now is the time to shift. Redirect your focus so that you're not repeating the same patterns, the same routines, after a loved one is gone. Enacting the same daily habits after a familiar face has left will keep you forever trapped in the pain of personal loss. And you are, of course, encouraged to keep their memory alive and establish a solid communication with them in the higher realm. But for the sake of your own well-being and personal progress, allow new potential to bloom into your life, too.

Hardships such as loss can catch us off guard and cause us grief. But we can learn to work with situations that arise by seeing beyond the moment and taking positive action. What grounds these actions even more and sustains our inner peace is establishing a connection with our loved one on the other side.

CARMEN

Connecting with Those Who Have Passed

Never an easy lesson of life, loss is experienced by all. And for those of us who have lost a loved one, certain days can become excruciating reminders of the people we miss terribly. After all, how are we to enjoy holidays, birthdays, and such without their presence?

Grief can easily work against us and weigh us down. That's because within our grief are a plethora of emotions mixed in: angst and anger and bitterness and betrayal. Grief draws out all those ugly monsters lying dormant within us. It's easy to create negative karma as we grieve, especially if the people around us are grieving as well. We are less patient, less tolerant, and less understanding. We disconnect from others and even ourselves—our bodies feel alien to us, as if day-to-day life were not real. After Virgil died, my daughter Alexandra and I were grieving in our own separate ways: she would lock herself in her room and want to be alone, while I needed constant affection and company around me. We were opposites in our grieving process, and we could have easily given in to the tension of having to bury our beloved or the frustration of clearing out the house of his belongings.

People often snap under the stress and pain stemming from loss. Naturally, it's harder to be there for each other when you and the other person are both feeling so much pain. Different people grieve differently, and the pain of grief can cause you to disconnect from those you love, which is why married couples who lose a child usually break up. This doesn't have to happen! After losing Virgil, Alexandra and I fought to come closer together than ever before. We realized that we had just lost the building block of our family, so we decided to become each other's foundation. We knew that if we didn't take care of each other during this hard time, no one else would. And we understood that if we separated, we would have no one to turn to.

If you and others are sharing grief, honor each other's grieving processes—showing compassion and patience for each other, even if you express grief or respond to it differently. Never say, "I'm hurting more than you are!" Grief is not a competition. Be mindful of the personal struggles of those around you, for they and only they know what they're feeling inside.

The most important thing to remember is that we can't heal ourselves—we must rely on others to get through the worst grief. You, like Alexandra, may be the type of person who just wants to be alone when you're upset. But when it comes to large-scale grief, this may not be the best idea. Being by yourself when you're a bit frustrated may help you meditate and release stress, but disconnecting from the world can turn into a dangerous behavior. It can perpetuate your suffering, throwing you further into angst and emotional struggle. It's critical to seek the comforting presence of others, at least for a little while each day, to distract your mind from your worry. This helps to reel you out from the depths of your pain, however temporarily. You may think you just want to be alone, but to transcend true grief, a comforting shoulder and ready ear are needed. Ask yourself if you want to be by yourself because that will most help you or because you are afraid of showing the depth of your sadness, anger, or fear. There is no shame in grieving deeply.

One way in which Alexandra and I conquered our grief was by being unafraid to bring up Virgil in conversation. Most people who grieve avoid speaking about the person they've just lost, either because it's too painful or because they almost feel like the loved one is now "off topic." Of course, when the suffering is fresh you don't want to add to your suffering by constantly talking about the person you lost or how much you miss him or her. But don't be afraid to bring up "that time when" for a few much-needed laughs with those around you.

Recounting memories of the person who's passed brings their presence back into your family, although in a different way than if they were there with you physically. It keeps your connection to them alive. And the thought that they might be there with you—smiling as you speak lovingly of them or chuckling as you remember some funny thing they used to do—can be very healing and comforting.

Acknowledging that your loved one never actually left is the first step to overcoming your grief. And as someone who regularly communicates with those who have passed over into the other realm, I assure you that your loved ones are still connected to you. The challenge is to stand up to the false idea that once they're gone, they're gone—that death is a final ending—and to accept instead that your loved one is ever present. You can feel their spiritual companionship more easily if you perform a few simple deeds each day.

Simple Ways to Connect to Your Loved One's Spirit

You do not have to be a medium to connect to your late loved one's spirit, although a medium can help you communicate with the one you lost. There are several ways you can contact that person on your own.

SPEAK TO THEM

Speak to your loved one as if they were next to you. Speaking without constraint allows you to release your emotions, relinquish tensions and fears, and establish communication. Your loved one's spirit will feel your yearning for them and, if possible, will come to you so that you can feel their presence. In the other realm, there's much to learn and do, but your loved one doesn't want you stuck in grief and will try to comfort you. You may not feel their presence right away, but if you are open to it, you might be surprised by when that special soul stops by to say hello in some way. So wish your departed one a good morning or a good night; remind them that you're making their favorite meal tonight or that the children are doing great in school. Speak freely. They are listening.

WRITE THEM A LETTER

Write your loved one a heartfelt letter allowing your emotions to transcribe through your words. Tell them everything and anything you want. Jot down your feelings, even if what you're feeling is guilt, anger, or bitterness. On the other side, they regret all the bad karma they created, so they will be glad that you are releasing your painful emotions and will try to comfort you and give you assistance in healing. Ask them for divine help—request their guidance on pressing matters in your life. You may leave this letter at their resting place, on their bed, or wherever you feel them most present.

WATCH FOR SIGNS

Even if you're a firm disbeliever in communication with the other side, suspend your disbelief just for once. I believe that the other side often tries to communicate with us through small hints that remind us that a world beyond our own does exist. Signs from the other side can include inexplicable noises in the house, flickering lights in a room, or randomly spotting your loved one's name on a sign. Be attentive for messages that you feel are not mere coincidences.

Believe in Their Love

Believe that love is eternal. Believing that this emotion can transcend any physical death will help you fill the void left by a missing person. Love never dies; it only changes forms. This means that as long as you are alive, that unparalleled love is alive within you.

Shift Your Mentality

The way in which we deal with difficult situations is greatly impacted by our mentality. If you choose to see physical loss as a tragedy, then it truly is. But if you understand that perhaps from the other side your loved one can help you in ways they could not in the physical world, then you begin to see their passing as a great resource of divine aid. Your mind-set shifts as you begin to accept your loss and muster up the courage to face it from an entirely different perspective.

Losing a loved one is nothing short of devastating. But take comfort in knowing that their spirit is eternal and omnipresent. By shifting your mentality and expanding your understanding, you can develop a strong connection with the person who is now a spirit in the other realm and actually feel their presence or influence.

And by experiencing loss, you can evolve in your family dynamic. Loss allows us to rearrange our priorities and form a new perspective. You can heal from family rifts in the present and toxic relationships that you are dealing with right now. If there is one lesson the grief of loss teaches us, it is that putting our egos before our loved ones is a costly mistake, and that we must appreciate each other for better or worse. After all, tomorrow is a hope, not a guarantee.

9

RELATIONSHIP CLEANSES FOR BETTER EMOTIONAL HEALTH

(Detoxify from Dysfunctional Relationships and Heal Family Rifts)

There are only two people you should compare yourself to: the old you and the you that you want to become.

—ALEXANDRA HARRA

Relationships that start out with the best of intentions and loving feelings can quickly turn toxic. It's difficult to change a dynamic when strong emotions are already involved, and even more difficult to escape from a toxic relationship when emotions have become warped. A toxic person may become obsessed and irrational, or even turn dangerous. They may no longer see a love situation logically.

Recognizing the signs that someone is emotionally toxic is not always easy. Often we meet people when they're in a good state of being and then, after we've grown attached to them, they show their true colors. We all put on our "best face" in the beginning, but time peels away that protective mask to reveal our insecurities and faults. Sometimes it's stress that brings out the worst in a person. Out of loyalty, we want to make the relationship work, remembering that person's potential for being good. The desire to hang in there through bad times is noble, but we can become badly hurt if we don't tread carefully.

Remember, the goal in relationships is to foster healthy, nurturing, uplifting human connections, and avoid poisonous relationships that drain you of joy and energy. When a relationship turns sour, pay close attention. If you listen to your instincts, you will know when to cut off someone whose obsession has become unhealthy. To find the strength and courage to go through with it, recognize your self-worth. Recognize, too, that you are doing the other person no favors by allowing the creation of bad karma between you. Let that person go their way and work on personal issues without you being enmeshed with him or her. And if it's you who is becoming too needy, clingy, or dependent on someone, you need to revisit what's within and find security in a relationship with yourself, your healthy ambitions and aspirations, and Spirit.

The relationships that most often become toxic are family connections. Relationships that build starting with birth and endure through every trial and phase of life weave powerful connections among people. Family rifts must always be addressed and healed, without the pressure of having to choose sides in a family argument.

We've experienced our fair share of family rifts in our own clan, and plenty of people have come to us for counseling on family matters, so we understand how hard it can be to bring healing into the household tribe. But the karma that arises from familial rifts is incredibly potent, which is why for your own karmic sake, no family relationship should be left up in the air. If you have no alternative but to walk away, you can at least do your part to heal the rift before resorting to that. Then you must heal that relationship within you by forgiving yourself and the other person (or people—sometimes, family rifts involve several members pitted against the rest of the relatives). Release the heavy, negative emotions around the memory of what transpired. Become a karma queen so you can free yourself of the karma even if the relationship is over.

We have a relative who got married several years back to a woman who was bad news—in fact, the entire family warned him about her. He didn't listen, naturally, since he was in love, and slowly but surely, this woman succeeded in breaking our relative away from his family. He was no longer allowed to see his siblings or communicate with his parents. He and this woman had a child, who was kept away from its grandparents and uncles and aunts. Sadly, this relative's father passed away last year, and the worst part of it all is that his father passed bitter, belittled, and broken-hearted at having lost the bond with his son because of the dark influence of a certain woman who was obsessed with keeping her husband all to herself. And it happens more often than you think.

The most unfortunate aspect of any toxic relationship is that it diminishes your ability to trust others. You can lose faith in other people and yourself and start to withdraw from people before you establish emotional intimacy. Trust is a delicate and hard virtue to recover once it's lost. If you leave your trust broken in pieces, all your future relationships will suffer. If you think you can bypass having trust in others and that this isn't a crucial element of a relationship, please listen: a stable sense of trust *must* be developed or you will drive people away—except those drawn to work through their own trust issues, and those are not the kinds of people you want to attract. Those people often lie and cheat, which means that no matter how vigilant you are, they are able to betray your trust. Therefore, you must resolve the issues of trust within you before they can be resolved outside you.

So how do you go about rebuilding the essence of trust? An easy way to remember is by using TRUST as an acronym:

T—Trust yourself unconditionally. The more you are honest with yourself, the more you reflect, and the more you connect with Spirit to remind yourself of your worthiness, the easier it will be to say no to relationships that can hurt you.

R—Return to a normal state of vulnerability rather than remain trapped in defensiveness or cynicism. Trust betrayed can rattle you, but by doing the work of forgiveness, you can reclaim your ability to trust. Don't be in such a rush to get over a betrayal that you skip the work of forgiving yourself for being so blind and the other person for being so cruel. Forgiveness is a process that takes time and work, but it's necessary.

U—Understand and have faith in the universal law of karma rather than fold to a desire for revenge or

manipulation. There is no power in revenge because engaging in such behavior simply creates more bad karma that will trap you.

S—Start from the beginning by forgiving those who harmed you in the past and detaching from unpleasant memories. When a painful memory comes up, explore the lesson you can learn from it. Review it as if it were a movie. What recurring themes do you notice? What was going on with the character who betrayed you? Did he have karma to work out? What could you do differently next time? Afterward, affirm your self-worth and say, "I forgive myself for making a choice that didn't work out well." Feel self-love. Then say, "God [or Spirit, or whatever term is comfortable for you], I give this person over to you. I no longer wish to share karma with this person."

T—Take time to build or rebuild a stable sense of trust rather than extend it instantly. The lesson of past betrayals is to become aware of your patterns and your karma so you don't rush into situations that will expose you to the same troubles you have experienced before. Know what you are getting into. Make a conscious decision about whether to work through your past karma via a relationship with this person or do it on your own and forgo a relationship with this individual. Even if you two share karma from a past life, you do not have to work it through with each other. Slow down and make better decisions about whom to trust.

To Leave or Not to Leave

I, Carmen, have seen endless rifts among my clients, from mother-daughter clashes to spousal feuds to longtime friendships that had turned noxious. Listening to thousands of cases and peering from the outside in, I have often thought, "Well, that could've been avoided." In most cases, rifts are self-made by people acting on their egos.

If you follow the voice of the ego that screams "me, me, me," of course you're going to damage the bond of "we." Once a rift has developed, it can be difficult to mend.

Sometimes it really isn't up to us to fix things, whether because it's just not our karma to heal the wound or because the other person is unwilling to put in the necessary effort on their end. I, Alexandra, had a friend named Irina whom I had known for many years. Somewhere in our early twenties, I observed that Irina was starting to change. She became involved with the wrong guy, began experimenting with drugs, and rearranged her priorities so that her looks were more important than her education. Irina also developed a weird, mild obsession . . . with me. She became jealous of my other friends and angry when I was not spending time with her, and she became more and more dependent on me for things she should have known how to do on her own by this age. The entire energy of the friendship shifted: we just weren't connecting anymore. The laughter, the mutual confidence in each other, and the easy communication were all gone. I felt something was wrong but also felt loyal to my friend.

When I tried speaking to Irina about it, she became defensive.

My words did not hold as much sway as the influences in Irina's life—new friends and a boyfriend who did not have her best interests at heart. I was trying to be a teacher friend, or even a soul mate friend, while Irina simply wanted a distractor friend. She did nothing to help improve the friendship or bring it back to where it was when it was healthy. So I did what I had to do and took a giant step back from a person who had once been a very close friend. Irina also distanced herself, seemingly with ease, though she did try to contact me when her boyfriend left her. At that point, I decided not to rekindle the friendship. I knew in my heart that our karma was finished. In other words, whatever Irina had to work out karmically, *it was not my job to work it out with her or for her.* My karmic lesson was to stop rescuing people who needed to rescue themselves. By focusing on my own karma instead, I realized I should simply let Irina work through her issues on her own.

It's funny that sometimes toxic relationships are such a burden to end. When there's lingering karma, they can make us feel like we're trapped in a net. But when the karma between them has been resolved, two people who used to have an intense relationship or were in each other's lives for many years can just walk away as if they had never met. Each individual may continue to have some of the karmic issues that drew them together, but the magnetic pull toward each other becomes so weak that they can walk away without remorse.

Our saving grace is developing a keen sense of when to be self-protective and leave a toxic relationship. You always have the choice to resolve your karma on your end without the other person around. Knowing when to hold on in the hopes of improving the relationship and when to walk away from the entire situation can be tricky. There are a six signs that it's definitely time to let go:

Sign number 1: Your intuition is nagging you to leave—you just feel it's wrong. Your gut knows—are you listening?

Sign number 2: You're being made to do things that make you very uncomfortable, favors and errands that the person should be doing for himself or herself. You find yourself doing things that you know are wrong in nature, things that can be detrimental to you or get you in trouble.

Sign number 3: You're being taken advantage of and it's become obvious (the other person is asking for money or borrowing your belongings). There's nothing wrong with helping out a friend, but when you're afraid not to—and this has happened before, or you see no signs of them getting on their feet again even after you rescue them—slow down. Think hard about what is happening between you and this person.

Sign number 4: Your energy is low. You feel exhausted and emotionally weak. If you find yourself dreading and avoiding someone whose company you once much enjoyed, pay attention. Relationships should nourish you, not make you feel as if your life force is being drained.

Sign number 5: You associate strong anxiety, fear, and worry with the relationship. Perhaps you panic when the person isn't with you or constantly worry that something will go wrong. When a relationship is marked by these emotions, it is not healthy for you.

Sign number 6: Your own progress and personal efforts are being hindered by the other person. Maybe you are doing so much for them that you have no time to attend to yourself. You find yourself setting aside your own goals and desires to tend to their most basic needs.

Appropriately dealing with a toxic relationship boils down to your safety, both physical and emotional. Of course, you should never stay in a relationship in which you're physically unsafe. It's definitely time to leave behind anyone who puts their hands on you! And this applies not just to a partner, but to a friend or even family member who is physically abusive or threatens to harm you in any way.

Protect your finances, also. People put on all sorts of disguises to access your trust and, later, your bank account. Be aware of who loves you unconditionally and who conditions their appreciation for you based on your money. Don't let the past cloud your view of the present. Often people will begin their relationship with you on their very best behavior, which will cause you to lower your guard.

And, of course, protect your children. Do not stay with someone who is rough with your children or who makes them feel uncomfortable. Once you have children, their well-being comes first.

Protect your emotional safety. Chronic stress leads to physical illness and disease. If you are having all sorts of physical ailments and are in an unhappy relationship, pay attention—your poor physical state may be the result of your tumultuous emotional state. You may well have karma to resolve.

Obsessed with the One You Can't Have

What happens when love becomes corrupt and negative emotions such as fear, anxiety, or anger creep in? The result is an adulterated version of love known as obsession.

None of us want to believe that we're obsessed with anything or anyone, but we're all a bit obsessed with something: it may be eating, or shopping, or spending time on the computer. Some people are workaholics.

When passion and focus snowball into obsession it's not good. Obsession is passion that's out of control. Even if you are obsessed with helping the world or spreading love, which are positive in essence, no thought or act should dominate your life to the point that you live only for it. Moderation is truly key: everything in moderation, nothing taken to an excess. This includes food, money, and even love and happiness. Life is meant to have some turbulence and uncertainty, sadness and even anger, yes. But when you take anything to excess, it's not healthy. You stop thinking clearly and begin to operate on autopilot.

It can be helpful to think about our habits from the perspective of the brain. The brain is like a school with many classrooms: one classroom teaches science, one philosophy, one mathematics, one writing, and so on. You are meant to take many classes, moving among the various rooms. If you attend only one class in one room, the other subjects are abandoned. The word *obsess* comes from the Latin verb *obsidere*, which means "to sit inside, or occupy." The person you are obsessed with figuratively occupies your brain and becomes your main concern, constantly popping up in your thoughts. If you're focusing only on a person you're in love with day and night, your thoughts are thickening what's known as neural networks in your brain, structures created and reinforced by thoughts. It's as if you're creating a groove that you can't get out of. It becomes harder and harder to break the patterns. They become imprinted on your brain and your karma and begin to determine your future because you are stuck in the same old classroom.

Wash That Man Right Out of Your Hair!

At the tender age of eighteen, I, Alexandra, experienced my first "real" relationship. And after six months, it was ended quite abruptly, and not by my choice. He said he just didn't feel the same way I felt for him, and I had such trouble understanding this. I continued to think about this person intensely for several months, until the desire died down. Was it because he had bruised my ego that I just couldn't let go, or had I developed a temporary obsession with him? I was also a teenager at the time, so I didn't have the same understanding as I do now. Now I would have respected his decision and sent him on his merry little way. I would've known that life goes on. But you'd be surprised to learn just how many obsessions linger for more than days and months and span into years.

And the people being obsessive are not sensitive teenagers or brokenhearted adolescents: often, they are adults, stuck on one person for whatever reason. All of us are drawn to reflect on relationships that end suddenly or not by our choice. We're drawn to think about how to improve a problematic relationship. It's natural to ponder on the why, when, where, and how. It's when the reflection becomes rumination as you go over memories again and again, learning nothing new, that you are beginning to obsess. Whenever any chapter of our lives comes to a close before we're prepared, we experience struggle in letting go.

The key to obsession is accepting that you can't have the person (at least, on your terms). A lack of acceptance is exactly what keeps someone totally bound to an ex-partner, or someone else's husband, or an estranged boyfriend who only sometimes comes around. In fact, it's what causes a person to obsess over the loss of a loved one. Even if you feel that person's spirit present in your life at times, you might become obsessed with him or her. That makes it difficult for the one who has passed to do the learning to be done in the other realm. Free yourself and the one you love from your obsession.

It seems the old phrase "you always want what you can't have" is true. And it's not just true of wanting to have unrealistic, tangible things—it's true of the people we want to have in our lives, too. We have to learn to end our obsessions and let them go. Let the thoughts leave your brain. To paraphrase the old song, wash that man right out of your hair already!

When it comes to obsession with people in this world, unfortunately, we are wired to seek and take on challenges. When a species is faced with environmental challenges, it quickly evolves to adapt to them. So subconsciously, we seek challenges as a means toward evolution and self-improvement. We are here to learn, but we can take a break from obsessing over a lesson! We don't have to stick with a relationship that is much too painful and difficult.

When someone has broken up with us or doesn't want to be with us, the challenge becomes to get them back. And our stubborn brains don't want to let go of this task until we've fulfilled it. All of us can relate, whether right now or at one point in our past. Is there someone you feel you must have a relationship with but who isn't available to you? How does this person impact your life? Could it be that you spend too much time thinking about him or her, or that you won't give up on this person even if they're not right for you or interested in having a relationship with you? Are you obsessed?

How do you distinguish between an intense love and an unhealthy preoccupation? How do you decipher when it's time to move on because the other person doesn't reciprocate your feelings? It becomes very difficult to answer these questions on our own when we're trapped within an emotional bubble, and it becomes all too easy to make the wrong decisions.

Answer the following seven questions truthfully. They will help you evaluate whether you are in fact obsessed with a person, whether your obsession is justified based on the other person's response to you, and whether you need to detach from the person on whom you're mentally dependent. I want you to introspect and be honest with yourself.

1. *How much of your day is taken up thinking about this person?* Is this person the first thing you think about when you wake up or the last thing before you go to sleep? Do thoughts of him or her suddenly float into your mind as you're working, socializing, or doing with other activities?

2. *What routine activities are interrupted by your obsessive thoughts?* Do you find you aren't engaged by your hobbies and interests lately? Perhaps you're avoiding other friends or family, or even neglecting your work.

3. *How strong are your feelings when it comes to this person?* If this person doesn't return your phone call or doesn't want to see you, do you feel emotionally damaged? Do you cry easily because of this person, and are you overly sensitive to his responses to you? Do you go back and forth between love and hate? If you become completely out of balance emotionally when you don't get what you want from this person, it can be a sign of obsession.

4. *Are your expectations realistic?* Do you expect to be with this person all the time even though deep down you know this will never happen?

5. *What is this person's response to you?* How does this person treat you? Does she make an effort to be with you or are you always the one to make the effort to get together?

6. *Are you hiding your obsession from those who love you?* Are you afraid to admit to anyone else just how much you dwell on this person? Do you have feelings of shame or embarrassment to confess how much you think about her?

7. *Where is this obsession coming from?* Were you traumatized by a breakup or damaged by a former relationship, which is making you not want to let go under any circumstance? Are there any deeply rooted insecurities or painful memories causing you to act this way?

Based on your answers, you may want to consider mentally and emotionally distancing yourself from the person in question. Perhaps what's really going on is something other than desire for this person—it could be the fear of loneliness or something else that has nothing to do with them and everything to do with you. There are effective ways to detach from someone, and the process doesn't have to hurt. Breaking free of obsession takes time and effort on your part. Here are five simple actions to take every day to help you detach from your obsession step by step:

Step one: Start your day with empowerment.

Say a quick prayer of empowerment each morning. Ask the Divine to make this a stress-free day and believe that it will be. Affirm to yourself as soon as you wake up that your happiness is not dependent on this person. Recite quotes that strengthen your independence and commitment to taking care of yourself and your needs. Instead of reverting your thoughts to this person, divert your attention by performing an activity centered on you and your own needs: exercise, go to the salon, get a massage, and so on. Perform any empowering activity that will refocus your attention on you.

Step two: Replace your obsession.

Exchange your obsession for a much more positive activity. Every time you find yourself thinking of the person, force yourself to have more productive, positive thoughts. Contemplate a project, think about an upcoming event that excites you, or evaluate the outcome of a different concern. Tell yourself that you have bigger things to worry about than that petty person. The more you force yourself to think about something else, the more you train your brain to function on other elements of life.

Step three: Turn to others.

This is not a time to isolate yourself. Rely on the support and compassion of friends and family, especially those who have experienced similar situations. It becomes easier to wean yourself off a person when you open yourself up to others and allow their energies into your life.

Step four: Practice self-care.

This is the time to take care of yourself. Invest in yourself and your needs. You are your own main priority. There's nothing wrong with a bit of self-pampering. Exercise regularly, take care of your health, splurge on one item, reinvent your look— anything to make yourself feel happy and confident in your attractiveness and worth! In this way, you learn to appreciate yourself enough to rise above the dominant influence of a single person.

Step five: Get into a new routine.

You need to distract yourself, even force yourself to look the other way when all you want to see is this person. You need to rewire the neurons in your brain so you stop obsessing. Daily activities help with this. Take up a new hobby, join a club— anything positive to fill your schedule. Don't give yourself time to obsess. Then make these new activities part of a new routine.

Like anything else in life, detachment takes time and is a process. But the results are remarkably liberating: a life in which an unhealthy obsession doesn't dominate your day-to-day thoughts and actions.

Obsession can contain a karmic component. Unresolved karma certainly draws us back to a person time and time again, even through different lives. Virgil used to tell me, Carmen, about a redheaded spirit who haunted him. The spirit had done this for many years. Apparently the woman was his spouse in another life and made her presence known to him. I felt her presence in our home on multiple occasions (talk about a pushy spirit!). She even appeared to me, claiming that her name was Julia and that she would "take back" Virgil, insisting, "He's my husband!" She also appeared to Virgil (who was the most skeptical person ever) in dreams. I heard Virgil mutter this woman's name in his sleep several times, saying, "No, Julia, I won't go with you." As Virgil was on his deathbed, I loathingly watched Julia float into the room wearing a strange smile of victory. This woman's obsession, obviously fueled by unresolved karma, went beyond her lifetime with Virgil and affected his present life—even though he had no interest in her and wanted to be free of her. A spirit such as Julia is troubled, unable to experience freedom and joy because she is weighed down by an obsession so powerful it transcends death.

Past-life connections can cause us to have an intense attachment to a person—and obsessions in this life can carry over to the next. Do not let yourself become trapped in one, or you might find yourself reliving the obsession in your next lifetime!

ALEXANDRA

The Sting of Rejection

The opposite of an obsession is a rejection or rift caused by someone who will not maintain a relationship with you even when you offer them freedom and acceptance. It's *so* painful when you can do nothing to keep that person in your life to any degree.

My aunt was always a somewhat distant family member, but she made her presence felt nonetheless. As a child, I became a giggly mess every time a package postmarked *Sweden* arrived in the mail: a large brown box brimming with toys, transporting familial love halfway across the world. It was all a little girl could ask for. I often wondered why my aunt chose to live in Sweden, but when she visited on holidays my curiosity diminished amid her endless hugs and innocent jokes. They say that scent is the strongest sense tied to memory. Mama Mona, as I called her, smelled of hand sanitizer and suppressed pain.

About seven years ago, Mama Mona announced her decision to relocate to the States. We were overjoyed and gifted her with an apartment to make her move as comfortable as possible. For several blissful months, Mama Mona participated in our lives in full force. My mother shared morning walks with her dear sister, my father discussed philosophy with his sister-in-law, and I cooked delicious vegan dinners with my aunt. To my small but love-laden family, the reunion was a dream come true.

We patronized a Greek restaurant on the night of my birthday. Spanakopitas and dolmathakia adorned our table as red wine was poured in abundance. I raised my glass and expressed my gratitude for another year of life and for the presence of my loved ones, especially my aunt who had returned to the family fold. I toasted to Mama Mona, the beaming woman sitting across from me, the beautiful, blue-eyed stranger about whom in reality I knew nothing. We shared the same nose, the same middle name, and the same obsessive love of writing. My joy of having the "prodigal son" return was short-lived.

Mama Mona vanished the next day. A handwritten note was left in her condominium, which she had transferred into my name unbeknownst to anyone. Her scribbles revealed that she felt she had made a terrible mistake and could not adjust to life here. We should not attempt to contact her again, she wrote.

I was devastated as I looked around what was now my condo. There was the familiar scent of hand sanitizer and suppressed pain lingering in the air, the only traces of my aunt left behind in her frenzy to leave.

I never heard from Mama Mona again, and perhaps I never will. I can't obsess about what we did or didn't do to make her go. We have no answers, and of course it was hard to let go of the questions "Why?" and "What could I have done differently?" Ultimately, we simply have to accept my aunt's rejection of us, her only family.

We all reject things on a daily basis: items we don't want, ideas we don't like, and opportunities we don't see fit. Rejection is as much a part of our world as is approval. But what happens when we as human beings reject each other?

Rejection comes as one of the most brutal stakes to the heart because it deals a direct blow to our ego. The ego is the inherent part of the self that holds intact our pride and self-esteem. We want to believe we can always fix what is broken and right what has gone terribly wrong. When the ego is bruised, a core element of our being is damaged. We often feel reduced to a lesser version of ourselves. We automatically begin the self-blame and assume there must be something wrong with us. Then we become angry at the person who rejected us, and then we swing back to trying to figure out again what we did wrong. We become a horrible pendulum of emotions.

I've learned to bear in mind the following two golden truths when feeling overwhelmed by rejection: don't take it personally, and see the rejection as an opportunity to evolve.

DON'T TAKE IT PERSONALLY

The only reason we suffer the sting of rejection is that we feel emotionally attached to a person. We truly believe there must be something intrinsically wrong within us to cause a person to dismiss us. It's natural to look inward and think, "I must be at fault." Yet often it has nothing to do with us. A person may be too busy or overburdened to devote attention and affection to us. She may have unresolved karma about emotional connections and intimacy and may not know how to involve us in her life without feeling pain. The person may fear rejection as a result of former experiences and automatically reject others to be self-protective. Remember that you never really know what goes on within someone's mind to draw conclusions about him or her.

When somebody completely cuts you off when you haven't done anything devastatingly terrible, it's because of that person's own insecurities and fears. It really isn't about you, or they would find a way to keep a cordial if limited connection. Take comfort in knowing that the person who rejects you is dealing with personal issues and that you most likely didn't do anything severe enough to cause their decision to break the bond completely and hurtfully.

When we feel rejected, we trap ourselves in a moment of doubt and distress. But we must learn to see past the fleeting period of pain and acknowledge that there is a higher purpose to not getting what we want in a relationship. That higher purpose is usually revealed in time. I, Carmen, have had many clients tell me that they felt awful when a love interest turned them away, but then they found the perfect partner when they least expected it. When that happened, they became grateful that they were rejected, or else they would've never met this new and better person. In retrospect, they may even be able to laugh at the fits of emotions the rejection invoked.

We all discover the greater purpose of our pain in due time. And the quicker we learn to see beyond the moment and trust that the Divine has a better plan for us, the quicker we heal from the sting of rejection.

For some children who were abandoned by a parent, rejection becomes a recurring challenge to conquer throughout life—a karmic issue. They may overreact when they feel turned down and not know that this is caused by a subconscious memory. Understanding the primary source of rejection and the impact it had on you can help you deal with this unpleasant emotion. Accept that this is not the first or last time you'll feel the ache of rejection, but that you've defeated this emotion before and will emerge stronger from each instance.

A person who rejects you is missing out on your inner and outer beauty. So why long to be with someone who doesn't see the full spectrum of your wonderful being? The next time you feel rejected, remind yourself of your amazing traits, your positive characteristics, and your invaluable qualities that undoubtedly exist.

SEE THE REJECTION AS AN OPPORTUNITY TO EVOLVE

Rejection does come with a positive side, as it gives us a chance to evolve. Rejection offers us an opportunity to evolve through and learn from our experiences. It allows us to look within and say, "Okay, maybe I can change this," or "Maybe I can fix that side of myself." After all, there is room for betterment in each of us, and sometimes it takes emotional anguish to be able to demolish the ego and come face to face with our truest self. If there is any constructive way to view rejection, it's through the lens of possibility: rejection offers the chance for self-improvement if we make an earnest effort to focus not on the loss but on what we might gain from within. We can become better, stronger, more powerful, more observant—indeed, there is much to be learned from rejection.

In the case of Mona, there was not much we could do. And you'll find that this is the case in many instances of rejection. We reached out to her time and time again, but she was completely nonresponsive. After months of trying, we felt we had done all we could. Had we continued to press her, we would have created negative karma between us, so we backed off and decided to let her be. We trusted that the connection between us will always be there, though it is not enforced through contact or communication.

You can't force people to be in your life. You have to make a solid effort to regain their presence, but if their rejection is persistent, you have to be wise enough to walk away. Pray for those who have rejected you, for their well-being and evolution. Let them go their own way and ask the universe to bless them. Continue to work on your own karma and on freeing yourself from any shared karma with the person who rejected you. Banish your guilt by reminding yourself that it wasn't your fault and that you did all you could to close out the karmic debt. Guilt attaches your karma to you. Forgiving yourself and the other person helps release the memory for good.

If you do want to reconnect with the person and think it's a good move, certain times may be much more conducive for a reconciliation than others. As we said in Chapter 4, it isn't a good time to reach out to someone if you or they are in a personal Year 9, but Year 1 is ideal to come back together. Calculate your codes to see if the timing is right for a possible rekindling of the relationship.

When you start to feel sad about a rift that could not be healed, or a person who has made it clear they want no more contact with you, remember the people you do have in your life—and start to make new friends as well. Everywhere you look, there are kind people looking to broaden their circle of friends and expand upon their supportive communities. You may be surprised at the marvelous relationships that are waiting for you.

10

CAN'T WE ALL JUST GET ALONG?

(A Little Neighborly Advice about Your Community Karma)

Speak softly. A yell is heard by many but understood by none. A whisper is felt in the heart by all.

—DR. CARMEN HARRA

Too many people have forgotten the importance of community, and we are only now beginning to realize that community really is inseparable from our well-being. Many studies show that having a strong social network is crucial for good health and leads to a longer life. Yet especially in the West, we are taught that individuality is key to success: we are supposed to be independent, live from our own earnings, and form our own opinions. In European and Latin American countries, however, community is the rudiment to a successful life. Community goes beyond family and close friends—it involves everyone from local shopkeepers to the neighbors on your block to people you meet online who share your interests and concerns. Being highly integrated in your neighborhood and in a community is a sign of a vibrant, healthy life.

In fact, being involved in a community is both an expression of our spirituality and a way of achieving practical, emotional, and spiritual support. We heal ourselves through positive interactions with family members, friends, neighbors, coworkers, and even strangers. We learn by watching and listening to the unique experiences of others. And if we practice compassion, we can build solid connections despite any differences.

By connecting with those around you, you can help heal the karma your community or family collectively shares. When we grieve, or when we're in trouble, we may look to the members of our community for support and be surprised by who shows up to help. It may be a community member we hardly know who comes to the rescue and leaves a lasting impression on our spirit. Whenever we perform selfless acts for members of our community, we create positive collective karma.

So who makes up your community? Think about every person you encounter on a regular basis, from neighbors to the cashier you exchange small talk with at the supermarket, to the buddies you bump into at the gym, to the peers you greet every morning as you enter your workplace. Your community can also exist online, and there's no reason your online and in-person communities can't blend. In short, your community is composed of the people who leave gentle footprints, however small, on your spirit.

Communities often share meaningful rituals that inspire

strangers to remember the value of creating bonds with others instead of remaining strangers. There's a row of houses in Boca Raton, Florida, that outdoes itself with decorations every Christmas. Literally every house on this block is adorned with a network of dancing lights, enormous ornaments hung from every nook, armies of festive figurines, and so on. People from all over South Florida gather on that street on Christmas Eve to be delighted by this local festival of lights. Florida doesn't normally "feel" like Christmas given the constant warm weather, but here, the visitors feel as if they've just stepped into Santa's workshop in the North Pole (well, a climate-controlled North Pole . . .). But more than just coming to take photos, people come to talk, to bond, and to give and receive each other's well-wishes and warm words. There are genuine smiles exchanged, handshakes of budding friendships, and children of all different ethnicities running after each other in play. It's as if those lights work wonders on the human soul, subduing all stresses and complaints, and extracting from within a kinship that's shared among family and strangers alike.

We watch this yearly event and think, "This is community at its best." It's an unfiltered celebration of community. And it's amazing how such simple joys can kindle a deep sense of connection that's intrinsic to us all. Whenever possible, attend your community gatherings and fuse your spirit with the different yet loving energies of others.

ALEXANDRA

Who's Behind That Social Media Page?

Nowadays, the Internet has become just as much a part of our community as anything else. My mom and I rely on social media to communicate with friends and family and build community. But Facebook, Twitter, Instagram, and the like can sometimes segregate people into groups instead of bringing them together as a whole. Too often, they create tension among us, and this doesn't have to be.

Some feel they have to portray a certain lifestyle on their social media pages: some people (especially women) feel they must look picture perfect, happy, and always well-off. At least, that's the trend I see in my generation. Social media can pit people against each other and lead to their feeling inferior because they don't have what others *appear* to have—perfect vacation photos, check-ins from expensive restaurants, and so on. Notice I said "appear": many people are not who they seem to be on social sites. They are deliberately cultivating an image that doesn't match their real lives. There's nothing wrong with making only positive events public, but don't mistake someone's cheery posts as a sign that everything is perfect in their world. Is everything perfect in yours? Probably not!

Make sure to check in with people in person, not just on social media. Get to know what's really going on with those you care about. One element of life we're quickly forgetting is that humans beings existed long before Facebook. Social media can actually diminish in-person social skills (which is ironic, given that it's supposed to be "social" media). We seem to know exactly how to post a captivating photo adorned with the right filter, smileys, and hashtags, but do we know how to give a rousing speech in front of a crowd? Do we know to look a person we've just met in the eyes, how to greet someone to make a good impression, or how firmly to shake their hand? No. The more we evolve via the Internet, the more we are dulled down in person. Beware of the effects of social media on your life. Having a lot of followers may grant you a new job opportunity, but it won't help you ace the interview. Limit your use of it. Have fun, and use it to your full advantage to expand your network, but don't become so absorbed in it that your interpersonal skills suffer as a result.

Whatever you choose to post on social media, you can make it positive, uplifting, and revitalizing—and reflective of your uniqueness. Don't be afraid to make your social media page a place where people can go to see and read good things for a change. People appreciate inspiration, believe me, and not just a pretty face or great body (although everyone loves a nice derrière). Share your ideas to improve this world and support others through your social media pages. It's demoralizing when a photo of my bum receives a hundred likes in seconds, while a photo of a well-versed quote receives just a smattering of likes. But I remain optimistic about using my platform to inspire people to think and feel more deeply.

To create good karma online, you must be careful of what you post and make public. Just as in real life, don't post things you know will have a negative effect on others unless you are willing to accept the karmic consequences. Ask yourself, would I say this in real life, in front of a rather large audience? Think about who is in your online community, and remember that more people may be able to view your page than you realize. Encourage positive dialogue and connections—it's fun to see two friends meet each other through your social media page and have a friendly exchange, but it's not fun to watch them lash out at each other over politics or other controversial topics. Have you ever read the comments below a political article online, for example? People are calling each other every name in the book. Why? Often, their identity isn't revealed and they feel no guilt in not insulting a person to their face. If they do use their real name and photo, they still feel they can get away with being disrespectful— because they're unlikely to meet the other posters in real life. But bad karma still gets created because negative energy is still being released into the universe. Don't write to a stranger online what you wouldn't say to them in person. There are respectful, intellectual ways to get your opinion across. After all, how do you know the Divine doesn't have Internet access, and isn't reading your crude comments going, "Tsk-tsk, there goes their good karma!"

In real life, if you act badly toward others, you create bad karma. Similarly, if your posts on Facebook, Twitter, Instagram, or other social sites are rude, conflictual, or unpleasantly confrontational in nature, you will create bad karma just as you would if you were abrasive to someone in person. You can choose to make public only positive things and still be that "cool" person everyone wants to follow. And you can become a karma queen by creating stellar karma in person *and* online.

Communicate Like a Karma Queen

Community and communication go hand in hand—in fact, both words share the same Latin root, which means simply "to share, divide among." When you communicate, you share words, emotions, ideas, values, and knowledge. Likewise, a community shares all of these ideals as well. Each time you speak, write, or communicate to or with another, you have the opportunity to generate positive or negative karma. Which will it be?

Positive, adequate communication lies at the heart of human interaction and at the core of a true community. There is nothing we can't achieve if we simply convey our thoughts in ways that are respectful of others as well as ourselves. It's important to talk through conflicts in a way that expresses what we need, feel, and think without necessarily hurting others. Having good communication in a community is key in bringing ideas to life and manifesting good intentions. After all, we can't work together if we can't communicate together. But when we do understand each other well, we can make miracles happen through joint efforts. Our mutual trust builds and we don't get bogged down in suspicion or gossip, factors that can brew hostility in a community.

We often choose harsh words over soft ones because we think they carry more resonance—we yell rather than whisper, assuming it'll get our point across. But what we don't realize is that yelling might be heard by all, but understood by none. It is the softer words that more easily penetrate the heart. We aren't as careful as we should be when choosing our words—or we speak them in a tone of voice or with body language that says, "I'm right and you're wrong. I'm hurt and you're to blame." Effective communication would eliminate arguments, misunderstandings, and strained relationships. There will always be times when someone offends you. Give that person the benefit of the doubt. Say, "I hate to bring this up, but . . ." or "I'm sure you don't realize, but . . ." before you express your frustration. Say, "I'm not sure I know what you mean by that. Can you explain?" Ask for clarification and assume the best intentions on the part of the other person. I promise that your relationships with people in general will be smoother if you choose softer, more productive words.

If you don't know someone well, it's especially important to be cautious in the words you choose. Avoid inflammatory language, and avoid expressing strong opinions that may intimidate or upset others. There is a time for exchanging ideas and opinions. It is not when you have just met someone in the community. Think about why you feel the need to "go there," into controversial territory, or express irritation or anger, to people you don't know well. Do they need to hear what you have to say, right now?

Different people require different approaches, which you need to keep in mind to communicate competently. You have to tailor your communication based on the type of relationship you have with someone, for starters. Knowing how to be a verbal chameleon results in truly effective speech. You aren't compromising what you are saying—you're just saying it more diplomatically, with sensitivity to that person's feelings and beliefs. This helps them better absorb your words, also.

Then too, be mindful of your communication with yourself. Yes, you are a part of your community, and even if you don't talk to yourself out loud, you talk to yourself silently! What is the quality of that communication? Do you berate or insult yourself, saying, "I'm so stupid"? Negative self-talk can be very destructive for you and for the people around you. You foster insecurity, jealousy, sadness, and anxiety when your self-talk is negative, and the people around you will pick up on these emotions and be affected by them. They will also receive the subconscious message that since this is your self-treatment, they can treat you in a similar manner.

Be loving and gentle in the language you use with yourself. You are a work in progress, so compassion is in order. The truth is that from the moment we are born, we begin to search for ourselves, and throughout our quest to "know thyself," we discover an endless number of aspects to our ever-evolving being. What you discover about yourself will not always make you happy, but whatever your flaws, know that if you didn't have those, you would have others. Besides, who you were a decade ago, a year ago, maybe even a day ago, is not who you are right now. We all grow and change by the second. And this calls for constant revision of perceived self-notions.

Uninhibited communication with yourself requires that you uncover the vastness of your needs, your strengths, and your weaknesses. Routine, honest introspection helps you recognize these traits. Ask yourself each day: What is it that I really want? Why? Is this need coming from my own heart or outside influence? Communicate to yourself in a loving way by affirming to yourself and the universe all that is good about you. Engage in a process of continual self-discovery and acknowledgment of your potential, and use your self-talk to reinforce your worth.

And while you are talking to yourself and others with compassion and kindness, don't forget the most important entity in your community: Spirit, the loving force of the universe. Establish a two-way communication with God. Sacred rituals such as prayer, meditation, and affirmations will help you plug in to a greater source of empowerment and receive messages about your life. Accept divine intervention and allow yourself to be shown what you must do. God tends to communicate through synchronicities and symbols, although you may "hear" or "see" words that are an answer to your inquiry to the Divine. Whenever you feel disconnected from others, remember that we are all children of God in one community. People care. They do, even when their egos don't let them show compassion. Spirit will make its presence known to you through people—sending a sudden messenger who reminds you that you are loved and cared for. This messenger may be a total stranger that you "randomly" meet who offers a helping hand or comforting words just when you have lost faith in people and God. We heal our karma through people, so God will send you just who you need to begin the process. Be open to the message and the messenger. You will feel more at peace, in harmony with the universe, and connected in your community when you make a point of talking to God and asking for guidance in healing karma and making better choices.

Yes, We Can All Just Get Along

In the heat of provocation from another, you can go one of two ways: you can succumb to the temptation of anger or you can rise above it. Being above negative influences lightens your spirit and expands your consciousness. You will become wiser and more placid. What once used to irritate, upset, or frustrate you will be reduced to mere dust you can simply brush off your shoulder. You will be able to see a broader perspective and not become bogged down in the petty tribulations of life. The next time you're caught in a situation that requires you to choose between peace or provocation, recite a few of these wise words in your mind:

You're better than that.

It's just not worth it to get upset.

Save it for your journal.

If you argue with someone, you stoop to their level.

A calm spirit lives a long life.

This won't be what you remember when you leave this world.

Take pride in being the bigger person.

Don't give someone else power over your mood.

You have more important things to do than engage in small spats.

It's more effective to send blessings than curses.

You were taught better.

You're too wise to give in.

You have larger battles to fight than this.

You will later regret what you say in the heat of the moment.

You could be doing greater things with your time than succumbing to conflict.

Sometimes, silence is golden.

This is not the first or last time this will happen.

Even in ugly circumstances, you always have a choice to create good karma. See provocations as opportunities to do just that.

CARMEN

Healing Collective Karma

Karma is not always individual. It is family and collective, and it can be shared among people, such as a family or ethnic group. Many of my clients declare that they're afraid to "meet the same fate" as their parents or other family members. This can mean ending up in divorce, suffering from the same illness, enduring similar financial hardships, and so on. They might call this a family curse, but I call it the family karma.

Karma is also very much alive in our community, country, or location. Earthquakes and hurricanes always develop in the same regions—this is the earth's karma. The same countries always go to war. The populations of certain territories always repeat the same circumstances. In Romania, as I mentioned earlier, we've developed a habit of assassinating our leaders because they were cruel and unfair to the people. We killed Decebal, Horea, Closca, Crisan, Yorga, and Ceausescu, among many other political leaders (don't worry about being able to pronounce these names as you read them). Sadly, throughout Europe, we became known for this hideous pattern.

Killing our leaders became embedded into the karma of Romania and its citizens. No matter how unjust the president or dictator, resorting to violence was not the right thing to do. By using violence to end our leader's reign, we only created a pattern—a pattern of having the next on the throne be just as corrupt. To a lesser degree, killing leaders is also part of American karma—presidents have been assassinated, and so have advocates for justice, such as Martin Luther King, Jr. There is a karmic price to pay for using violence to solve our problems. It not only does not solve our problems, it perpetuates them.

Healing collective karma begins by analyzing our individual karma and its role in the greater karmic scheme: What is my karma, and how is it contributing to the whole? Do I have positive or negative karma? We all have a little bit of both, but which karma are you forcing upon others? Ask yourself, do I act to heal the karma of my group, or do I continue to act on its negative cycle?

Good Deeds, Good Karma

Whatever your connection to others—whether you are a relative, friend, neighbor, or stranger—you are at your best when you give your best to them. A strong community is formed and maintained when members strive to be compassionate in their communications and interact in ways that respect everyone, including themselves. Many of us take great pride in being virtuous, but our virtues are worthless if kept to ourselves. So many people can benefit from your gifts and talents, and likewise you can benefit greatly from theirs. The Bible says, "Don't hide your light under a bushel." Extending your excellence, letting your goodness radiate, causes a ripple effect of consciousness. You see good, and you do good—then others see you do good, and they do good. This chain of connection and influence is called inspiration. You inspire or breathe the breath of love into others when you use the abilities that come naturally to you to serve those around you.

When you set an example of creating pleasant karma and resolving the bad, you will begin to notice that the people around you start to change their thoughts, intentions, and actions. And not just in their own lives, but in their treatment of you: they respect you more. We're quick to share our opinions and complaints with the world, but if we focused instead on sharing our virtues, perhaps we would resolve our communities' problems much more easily.

ALEXANDRA

Virtues to Share with the World

A few months ago, our twenty-year-old cat, Bebe, passed away quite suddenly. Bebe lived a long and healthy life, and I was well aware when her time to go drew near, but I still lamented her death for weeks. There was something special about Bebe, a certain curious way in which she sat at the foot of my bed and simply stared at me, as if her sparkling black eyes were abounding with the secrets of the universe.

As any animal lover will say of their pet, Bebe was more than a cat. She was my secret inspiration. Bebe had aged into a little old lady in front of my eyes, and with her years came an inevitable inheritance of wisdom. My mom and I are convinced that the spirit of my late grandmother, Sanda, had transmigrated into Bebe so as to remain close to our family (I promise you we are normal . . .). I know—she was "just" a cat. But I truly believe our pets come into our lives to teach us what we are too stubborn or perhaps too blind to see otherwise. Their unconditional love opens our eyes to truths we might otherwise miss. After all, animals are members of our community, too. Here are five virtues Bebe taught me that help me be a better person and deliver kindness and compassion to everyone I meet.

Presence

Our presence alone can be a virtue. When we offer our presence to someone in need, we may not even need to give advice. Listening may be all they need to feel loved and comforted in times of difficulty. Bebe instinctively knew to lie right next to me whenever I wasn't feeling well. Her silent yet powerful presence soothed me. The next time someone reaches out to you with a problem, simply give them a bit of your time, a small piece of you, and know that this can make a world of a difference. Instead of being frustrated by the neighbor who loves to talk, take a few minutes out of your busy day to listen with full attention. Make eye contact. Relate their story to your own life— maybe you can learn something, or there's a bigger reason you're hearing what you're hearing right now. Your kind act will create worthy karma and your presence will bring a glimpse of sunshine in another person's day.

PATIENCE

Bebe would wait in the kitchen for hours until we got home to feed her. She never whined or became distressed. She simply waited. In our own lives, we can incorporate patience by understanding that *it's okay to wait*. It's okay to let someone else go in front of you, it's okay to wait for someone who's late, and it's okay to make mistakes until you get it right. Practicing small instances of patience helps bring about patience in the larger elements of life. Remember also to have patience with yourself. Respond to others' ignorance with patience and you will grow to understand their actions. Remember to be patient the next time you are in traffic, or stuck in a line, or irritated because you have to explain something to someone who should already know how to do a certain task by now. Take a breath and affirm silently, "I am creating consistent good karma by being loving and patient."

DEVOTION

A step above loyalty, devotion is the art of undying dedication. Bebe demonstrated devotion by never straying from the house. Show your loved ones that you are devoted to them: your spouse, your children, your friends, the people in your community, and so on. A large part of devotion is continuing to display loyalty even when someone has let you down. Don't give up on others so easily—your devotion to them will be rewarded in time. When members of a community are devoted to the good of the whole, that community thrives and grows.

OBSERVATION

Bebe grew immune to her five rambunctious housemates, a community of cats and dogs that was sometimes harmonious and most times cacophonous. As they wrestled and warred against each other, Bebe kept her distance and surveyed the other animals' behavior with quiet tolerance and acceptance. She helped me see that the best way to detach from conflict is by choosing not to become involved in it in the first place. At times, it's best to observe and not engage. We must see the world around us through peaceful and nonjudgmental eyes, choosing to learn from outside battles rather than participate in them. Right now, our world is racked by anger and roiling emotions. We can engage it by becoming angry ourselves, or we can quietly observe people's behavior and ponder what is driving them without getting pulled into the general unhappiness and misery trapping others. To keep your distance is best for your well-being.

HEALING

We have an extraordinary capacity to heal each other, though we rarely use it. Our ability to heal is delivered to others through a simple and underrated method. It's called love. And if it's unconditional, it can help us overcome our greatest challenges. Bebe continued to love me through my woes and worries—her degree of attachment wasn't influenced by my appearance or finances. Though you may not always receive it in return, practice unconditional love to help elevate and spiritually nourish the people in your life. Even if you just pick up something a stranger has dropped, or share a smile, or joke about the weather, you play a small part in healing the troubles in this world because you create honorable karma in that moment. You don't have to take on all the problems of the world and become overwhelmed, but at least become aware. You simply have to do what you can each day.

Virtues have to be shared to be felt. If you isolate yourself because people have disappointed you in the past, and you spend time with only your pets who love you unconditionally, pay attention to what these precious animals are teaching you. You aren't meant to be alone, nursing your hurts. You are meant to create harmony and exceptional karma with others. Draw strength from your community of pets, but then go out into the human community, knowing that imperfection will be found. Extend your highest virtues, your greatest parts of yourself, and gift them to the world to feel them grow in your heart. Open up and trust, and don't be surprised when someone unexpected reminds you that people do care, will go out of their way for you, and often give while expecting nothing in return.

CARMEN

The Count of Human Compassion

We are unified in our community through acts of compassion, of giving without expecting to receive and doing for the sole sake of doing good. But unfortunately, on many occasions, we feel alienated from each other. We can be distrustful or even suspicious, particularly if we don't know someone well—or have heard only about their shortcomings and not their strengths. We can prejudge others based on what we've heard or read "people like that" are like. The mind is very good at creating fear and distrust, which erodes our ability to participate in our community in a positive way that nourishes us and others.

If there are miracles in the world, perhaps the most miraculous one of all is compassion. It can melt divisions between people instantly. When a natural disaster strikes, the most aloof and cynical person can be found risking his own safety to help another and speaking words of hope and kindness. The source of the greatest miracles can be our own compassionate heart.

Recently, I've suffered mysterious bouts of high blood pressure. I went completely against doctors' orders and thought I would be fine on a six-hour flight from Florida to Los Angeles. After the first hour, however, I felt my blood pressure begin to spike. I suddenly realized I was stuck on an airplane, flying alone, and with no medical resources available for hours. I began to panic. The pounding in my head and chest mounted. It was intolerable—the airplane cabin began to spin and my vision turned blurry. What a mistake I had made! In an act of desperation, I hit the call button and blurted to the flight attendant that I wasn't feeling well. What I encountered next forever solidified my belief in the human potential for performing good. The flight attendant, Annie, darted to retrieve an oxygen tank and some ice. She quickly placed an oxygen mask over my face, held ice to my forehead, and began to measure my blood pressure. Most notable of all, Annie held my hand and spoke softly to me, reassuring me that I would be just fine, as if she had known me for many years.

For the following four hours, Annie did not budge from my side. When she became tired of standing, Annie sat on the floor, but her hand did not release mine for a second. It wasn't the medical help I would receive in a hospital, but Annie helped me in a very different way: she showed me unrestrained compassion. And that to me made all the difference in the world when I was feeling my most scared.

Every passenger who walked by my row expressed their sincere concerns and hopes that I would feel better soon. It was their tender smiles, the crinkles around their eyes, and the authenticity of their few but true words that did make me feel better. My heart rate slowed noticeably. I began to have faith that I would be okay. I lost count of how many people showed me compassion on the flight. It radiated from the human spirit, brilliantly and unconditionally as unapologetic kindness often does.

We are capable of changing each other's lives if we unlock our compassion. People will upset you, hurt you, inconvenience you, and even betray you. We all possess a fountain of clemency within us. Yet we build a self-protecting dam around it. We fear that allowing our compassion to flow freely may make us vulnerable to others and we'll be hurt, so we keep our heart well walled, preserving our compassion for some other, future day. But compassion doesn't operate this way. It dies quietly inside us, snuffed out by our fear. What a waste of this beautiful, innate capacity.

Ultimately, life ushers us all through the same lessons, trials, and misfortunes. Life is not a comparison game, where my pain is bigger than yours, or her victimhood is greater than his. What has happened to another has happened, is happening, or will happen to you in some form or another. Suffering has the same quality no matter who experiences it, and the same ability to destroy a person's faith. Do not succumb to measuring your suffering against another's. Instead, let compassion rise within you—compassion for yourself and compassion for other people, even those who have hurt you. In this way, you can soften your heart and open to the immeasurable love that is available to you.

Because we are kind and vulnerable does not mean we are gullible, weak, or dumb. It means we are evolved. I have been taken advantage of often—sometimes, shamelessly. I regret not listening to my heart when it told me to reserve my trust given the signs that all was not right with a person whose unresolved karma would lead him or her to hurt me. And yet I don't regret the person I was when I loved and accepted those who later did me harm. I can be proud of the kindness I let flow from an open heart. I remind myself of that whenever I'm tempted to obsess over someone who took my money, betrayed my trust, or broke my confidence. Karma has a way of balancing everything, so there is no need to hold on to anger or resentment toward others. Doing that closes the heart to love, and the only person that hurts in the long run is *you*.

Regardless of how much you have been hurt in the past by people whom you opened yourself to, love again. Disable your anger. Being irate is the antithesis of being compassionate—it narrows our understanding, dulls our awareness, and stifles our logic. When we allow ourselves to become frustrated over every little injustice done to us, we invite anger to dominate more and more of our life experiences. Soon, we become the agent of our anger, acting out in ways that only suit its purpose. Eliminate this emotion by always reminding yourself, "It's not worth becoming angry over." By stopping anger in its tracks, you invite others to release themselves from the grip of anger, too. Communications improve. Communities improve. Then we can finally reach solutions to the bigger, more complex problems that plague us.

Like the flight attendant who held my hand for hours, you can extend compassion without reason or expectation. This, truly, will make you a better person. You begin to see differently when you view the world through the lens of positive intent. Love fully. Don't be afraid. If someone rejects your love, that person probably has unresolved karma—say a silent blessing and move on. Tend to your own karmic garden and see to it that it blooms luxuriously.

The count of human compassion is endless—immeasurable. We can live out the joyful, harmonious communities and the fulfilling, happy lives we seek if we will only break down the empathetic barriers within us and allow ourselves to feel more and doubt less. Then, then, you will be capable of unimaginable good, both for yourself and for others, and perform small but overlooked acts that leave permanent impressions on the soul.

What a world we will share then, when our karma is resolved!

ACKNOWLEDGMENTS

I would like to thank everyone who believed in the potential of this book: my agent, Devra Jacobs, who told me over and over again that we can make this happen, and who worked tirelessly to find me just the right publisher for my project. I am grateful to Penguin Books, of course, for this incredible opportunity and to Joel Fotinos, who allowed me to share my karmic message with the world. I'm thankful also to the gifted editors who perfected my writing, especially Andrew Yackira. And last but not least, I would like to honor the tens of thousands of clients I have seen over the last twenty years—the individuals who trusted me both to peer into their personal problems and celebrate in their deepest joys, and who each contributed a tidbit of insight toward my understanding of the miracle that is the human bond.